Raised by Miracles

CRISTINA LITVIN

To Skye, my heavenly team, and my earthly team: you know who you are.

Foreword

Just because you have not had the experience does not mean that it does not exist.

I do not want to misrepresent this story. The story you are about to read is full of paranormal phenomena and is not for the faint of heart.

It is absolutely a true story, and nothing has been fictionalized. However, some names have been changed to protect the privacy of those involved.

I am a spiritual warrior here on a spiritual mission, because of this unseen forces have relentlessly attacked me most of my life.

I do not wish to change anyone's spirituality. Let me be very clear about that. This is not a come-to-Jesus book.

I am not a writer. I am a person of very humble means and limited resources, as it is very difficult here on Earth to lead a spiritual life outside of religion. English is not my first language. This is no literary work of art.

I'm a flawed human with limited gifts and limited means who simply does her best.

Despite witnessing many miracles, I remained a skeptic until I met others like me. I do not begrudge anyone who does not believe me or agree. We are all here to have our own journeys. I most certainly respect yours. I am just stating the facts of what happened to me.

The story you are about to read is about the miracles it took to keep me alive, about trusting the process, and about getting the truth out there about people like me. I have been given many labels, such as: incarnated master, incarnated yogi, divine being, shaman, psychic, the keeper of the twelfth realm, empath, sensitive, and more. Professional psychics say I am much more than an empath. I scored a perfect score on Dr. Judith Orloff's empath test.

I am not comfortable with labels, as I feel they are divisive. The only label I have been remotely comfortable with has been 'spiritual warrior.' We are all equal under God's eyes, so labels, to me, are a human concept. Anyone can join God's army. Being a spiritual warrior is open to all, which makes me comfortable using that term.

To be a spiritual warrior, you need a sincere desire to seek the truth, a strong physical body, a commitment to be honorable, to keep your spirit strong by staying away from addictions, and to do the right thing at every opportunity presented to you in life. But the most important is putting God, Yahweh, first. Yahweh is your best friend. At my Awakening I asked what God truly is because I knew it was not a white bearded man up in the sky. The answer I got was, "The Creator of this universe is something so complex that it is not possible for the human mind to process it."

To me, it does not matter what you call It, Him—be it Yahweh, God, Elohim, Allah, Adonai, or flying spaghetti monster—as long as it is done with good intentions. There is so much about our Creator that humans have misconceptions about.

My intention is not to change anyone's spirituality. My interest is in letting folks know that the things I witnessed are possible. If I had been aware, my life would have been completely different.

I have met something that identified itself to be The Creator in this realm, in this reality. I know it sounds farfetched. Please read my story. I pray that the truth will resonate with you.

I wrote this book in my voice because something that identified itself to be The Creator asked me to never change my personality. I feel that if this book were written in someone else's voice, perhaps the honesty behind the words would get lost.

That is the spirit with which I wrote this book. It is what it is. I know many will call me a liar, a con, or an abomination. I have to follow what my soul requires of me. My soul requires that I write this book.

CHAPTER 1

A Strange Life from the Beginning

My name is Cristina. Yes, just Cristina. My mother didn't think a middle name was important. My parents named me after my grandmother, Christina. In 1977, when I was born in Spain, there was a rule created by dictator Francisco Franco that all children born on Spanish soil must receive a Spanish first name. Adhering to the rule, they took the 'h' out of my name. The combination of the letters 'c' and 'h' in Spanish would not produce the proper sound, my name would no longer be 'Cristina'. It would sound more like 'Chee-stina'. In Spanish, the CHR in Christina breaks a grammar rule that you can't have three consonants in a row. So, Cristina with no 'h' was the name my parents went with.

My life has been full of strange events. Through all of it, I kept an open mind.

This book was written through my own unique perspectives, beliefs, and experiences. I mean no harm. I am telling this story to the best of my understanding. Like every human on Earth, I have erroneous beliefs, both spiritual and human concepts.

My promise is to be honest and forthcoming while sharing everything to the best of my memory. I ask that you please keep an open mind and heart. Try not to judge what you are about to read. We are human, and judging is natural to us.

~

Bill and Ina met two years before I was born, in 1975. Ina liked to play cards and had discovered that the Holland Club played bridge once a month. The Holland Club was an expat social club that met several times a month. Expats are former citizens of a foreign country. Dutch citizens would regularly convene at a local hotel in Benalmadena, Spain, for the Holland Club. My mom and dad were paired as bridge partners. Bill, my father, was the proprietor of a hotel and restaurant on the outskirts of Amsterdam's red-light district; my mother, Ina, owned a fruit and vegetable import and export company and did business throughout Europe. Ina was married to a Spanish man. She had two daughters, one named Hazel from a previous marriage, and the other, Nicole, with her Spanish husband. Bill was single.

I could write an entire book about my amazing father. In 1941, at seventeen, my dad started asking Dutch farmers to take in Jewish children. He did this work for an organized group called the Jewish Underground. My father had married a Jewish girl. They had a daughter named Anja. The town's doctor, my grandfather, Gustaaf, also acted as the backup veterinarian in case the local vet had multiple calls, was unwell, or was on leave. Bill became familiar with many farmers, as he frequently accompanied Gustaaf on these calls. Most farmers had ten or more children; one family even had twenty-four! My father successfully convinced many farmers to take in one or two Jewish children.

In 1943, the Nazis caught up to my father. They took him and his wife to different concentration camps. Eighteen months after being taken as a POW (prisoner of war), he escaped the camp. He made his way back to the Netherlands and to his childhood home which was occupied by the Nazis.

My grandfather, the doctor, had a large home, which was also the location of his practice. This home held a secret panic room where there was a bed, a pot, a desk, and a chair. The room was so small, you couldn't stand. My father spent six months in that situation before the war ended. Fortunately, his childhood nanny was still there, providing him with food and cleaning his pot. After the war, he discovered that both his wife and daughter were dead.

Despite my dad's open flirting, Ina stood firm in her claim that she was deeply in love with her husband. In fact, she was so committed to her marriage that she even suggested bringing him along the next time they played so that Bill could meet him. Ina made plans for the following month to bring her husband and her daughters to meet Bill. The family could spend an enjoyable afternoon by the hotel's pool, while Ina played bridge.

After the card game was over, Bill and Ina sat at the bar chatting as that had become routine for them after bridge. Bill began, "Ina, I don't know how to say this..."

Ina asked, "What's wrong, Bill?"

"I am pretty sure your husband is having an affair with your oldest daughter." My dad was old-fashioned and spoke directly.

"Impossible, I would know!" Ina was indignant.

"If it's not too much trouble, could you do me a favor and go home to confront your daughter? I am certain of what I saw, but if I am mistaken, I will offer you my sincerest apologies." Bill explained he had been a sexual crimes detective in the city of Amsterdam for twelve years. This made Ina pay attention. My father never revealed exactly what he saw. He would always explain it as an inappropriate exchange that he caught between them.

As soon as my mom went home and asked Hazel about it, she admitted to the truth without hesitation. When she confided in my mother, she was already fifteen. She revealed the problem started when she was only nine years old. He plied her with alcohol and money to keep her quiet.

Sadly, Hazel fell into the depths of alcoholism and never recovered.

My mother acted quickly. She called my father right after discovering the news. He directed her to call the authorities. The cops arrested the child molester.

Afterward, my dad insisted on dating my mom, but she was reluctant. She was going through a lot. Not only had her daughter been molested, but my grandmother, Christina, was dying. During my grandmother's final moments in the hospital, she gave some advice to my mother. She told her to marry Bill. She believed he would take good care of her.

Bill and Ina's decision to get married was not the only significant decision they made. After selling both their businesses, they planned to retire and start a family. My parents bought a house in Torremolinos, Spain, also known as La Costa del Sol. With four bedrooms and a spacious kitchen that perfectly suited my parent's passion for cooking, the house was perfect. The property had enough space for both a pool and an extensive orchard and vegetable garden.

Because of my mother's difficulty with conceiving due to age, she planned to go back on the pill if she couldn't conceive in the next month. The miracle of my conception happened then. I came into this world on March 28, 1977, after my mother went into labor during a card game. Whenever we went to Clinica Santa Elena (the hospital where I was born), I always felt a rush of butterflies in my stomach. When I was born, I was sunny side up. My mom had a difficult time as the placenta got stuck to her. She had to wait for hours until an anesthesiologist was available to administer sedation.

Even as a baby, I had fully formed adult thoughts and understood everything happening around me, though I wasn't able to talk. One day, at fifteen months old, I was out by the pool while my sister, Nicole, was doing dishes. Her friend, Chantal, was watching me. While Chantal was dozing off by the pool, a voice spoke to me as clear as day urging me to jump into the swimming pool. Even though I couldn't speak, I understood everything.

I jumped in. As I was sinking to the bottom, a female voice came on and said, "Stay calm, everything is going to be okay." A warm blanket of comforting energy surrounded me, and then I could breathe water as if it were air. Even at fifteen months old, I knew a miracle had just happened and was able to remember most of it.

While I was lying motionless at the bottom of the pool, Nicole noticed me and, without hesitation, dove in to rescue me. I can still remember what it felt like being at the bottom. In the years that followed, every summer I attempted to breathe water as I had done before, which resulted in excruciating pain in my nose. The memory of what happened in the pool remains vivid in my mind even today.

My parents enrolled me in a preschool after I turned two, despite not being employed. The duties of taking care of a toddler quickly over-whelmed my parents. The preschool was not thrilled. The director fought my mom tooth and nail because I didn't speak Spanish, only Dutch.

"That is precisely why we are putting her in preschool," my mother affirmed. "She will learn Spanish in no time!"

Like most schools in Spain, Catholicism was the foundation for this preschool. There I would learn a unique version of the Lord's Prayer that has always allowed me to dial into Heaven like a 911 call. I also learned to deal with extremely mean teachers at this school. They would even threaten us with scissors and with cutting out our tongues. In those moments, I would hear telepathically, "They don't really mean it." I would remain calm. My inability to speak the native language led to daily punishments, as I couldn't comprehend the instructions. Because of this I was made to stand in a corner for hours every day. I would go into what I would later in life come to know as meditation.

One day, I had a strange experience at my preschool where some-thing came to me telepathically and said, "Today we are going to intro-duce you to the concept of jealousy. Do you see that girl over there? Would you like to have her beautiful pencils?"

I replied, "No, I wouldn't. Look how happy they make her."

Then they pointed at a girl and asked, "Isn't she beautiful? Do you wish to be that pretty?"

I answered, "I am truly so happy for her that she is so pretty. What a blessing!" Did I mention I thought as an adult from shortly after birth? I was born already on my path to Enlightenment.

"Fine, how about Miriam? Do you see how popular she is? Don't you wish you had friends like her? Everyone wants to play with her." It was at that moment that I realized something. I was envious of her and the friendships she had.

"Yup," I thought to myself. "I wish so badly that I had friends like her." This was the first time in my life that I had ever experienced envy. Following that day, Miriam and I had the opportunity to get to know each other and developed a friendship. I believe that angels had a hand in that. I asked my mom to invite her to my birthday party. Miriam's mother was British. Ina was fluent in five languages, including English, so the two mothers quickly developed a rapport with each other. I couldn't understand a word of what they were saying, but there was a big commotion and much laughter between the two of them.

"It's almost unbelievable, but Miriam and you were both born on March 28th! And the doctor who delivered her was the same as yours— Dr. Cano!" I was stunned.

"I'm sorry, sweetheart, but Miriam is having a party the same day. She is also very sad she can't come, but next year we are going to plan the birthdays so you can be at each other's parties." That was indeed the case every year until we were nine. We lost contact after that. The bond we shared was truly special, and it led to many sleepovers filled with laughter, joy, and a deep sense of connection.

A new student named Fabio joined our preschool after I had been there for about a year. Fabio and I had an instant connection. From that day on, we would play together almost every recess. One day at home, I was riding my tricycle up and down our long driveway. When I arrived at the gate, it startled me to find Fabio at the house directly across the street from ours.

"Fabio! What are you doing there?"

He answered, "I live here."

I jumped off my trike and ran to my mom. I almost had a panic attack, trying to get the words out of my mouth.

"Mom! Mommy!!! Mom, remember the boy I have been telling you about from school? Fabio?"

"Yes."

"Mom, he lives across the street!"

"What are you talking about?" my mom asked.

"I went out back and there he was. Mom, can you ask if he can come over to play?"

My mom, who was still in disbelief, went out back and confirmed that Fabio and his family had indeed moved in several months earlier.

Around the age of four, many strange things started happening. It began with me riding in the front seat of my dad's car. There were no car seats back then. One time when the door swung open, I fell with my torso hanging halfway out. Of course, my father immediately stopped the car to make sure I was okay. I was fine, but I felt the presence of what I now perceive as something sinister which had opened the door.

A few months before that, I found myself gasping for air after attempting to swallow Jamon Serrano (a cured ham similar to prosciutto). As I was struggling to breathe and my lips were turning blue, my intuition was urging me to remain calm. My mom tried to retrieve the ham to no avail. I knew even then that an angel came up with this solution: "Nicole, your hands are smaller. Please try to get it out," said my mom. Nicole, once again, came to the rescue and got the ham out.

I used to have these vivid and realistic dreams where I would soar through the sky with what I perceived to be angels by my side. So much so I asked my friends, "You guys go flying sometimes, right?" My friends explained to me that I was dreaming, but man did it feel real. Periodically, at my preschool, the same female voice that spoke to me during my swimming pool incident, would come to visit me. She introduced a breathing game during our first meeting. The game involved inhaling deeply, holding my breath, which would transport me to other realms where I saw different things. My body would be filled with what I felt as divine energy the moment I got back.

When I was two, my parents planned a trip to the United States to visit both grandfathers.

Jan Voormolen, my maternal grandfather, was an exceptional man. I called him my 'Opa'. Following his retirement as the millionaire owner of a family construction company started by his father and later shared with his brother, he made a real estate investment and purchased a condo in Pompano Beach, Florida. Jan Voormolen oversaw the building of bridges and buildings throughout the Netherlands. The foreman on their jobs was Jewish. He was also my Opa's closest friend. They were so close they even lived next door to each other, sharing a wall. Nowadays, the term row house is known as a townhouse.

In response to the start of the war, these men constructed a concealed compartment that was between their neighboring homes. They built the compartment in such a way that they could only open it from the inside. When it was in use, it just looked like an ordinary wall. They always left it ajar with a stick when not in use. This decision was proven wise as one day the Nazis paid a visit to their homes. They went into hiding as soon as the soldiers, who had showed up in a tank, began questioning my grandmother.

"We know they are in there. We know they went in and did not come out. Tell us where they are or I will blow your baby right out of your belly!"

The soldier, with his weapon drawn, had it aimed directly at her stomach when he made the statement. My grandmother, Christina, was visibly pregnant. They proceeded to blast the chimney with the tank under the assumption that the men were inside. Christina stood strong. Eventually, the Nazis gave up.

Christina loved Jan like you see in the movies. Even after their eventual divorce, she never had a relationship afterwards, always hoping he would come back to her. Love kept her from enjoying the rest of her life. Her inability to move on and dependence on alcohol would consume her. She died of cirrhosis of the liver.

Eventually, the Nazis forced the Jewish foreman and his family into a concentration camp. The memory of the little girl coming over to give all her toys to my mother, saying she wouldn't need them where she was going, is something that my mother said she would never forget. No one ever heard from the family again.

There is real evil in this world and those who indulge in it.

~

That summer, my family and I embarked on a cross-country trip to Santa Rosa, California, with the purpose of meeting my paternal grandfather, Opa Gus. My grandpa followed in the footsteps of his father and became a doctor, continuing the family tradition. He was a town doctor in Langbroek, the Netherlands first. Then, after the war ended, he worked as a ship's doctor for the Holland America cruise line. His wife had left him in 1933 for another woman, so he had nothing to hold him back in the Netherlands. After meeting Margaret, an American divorcée, he married her and they remained together for the rest of their lives. They settled into their new home in Santa Rosa, California. He started working as a researcher at a genetic laboratory. By his account, he made a groundbreaking discovery of the hormone responsible for cows' accelerated growth. He claimed the U.S. government came in, stole his research and gave it to corporations.

The divine energy that existed between my grandfather and I was something extraordinary. I felt it every time we came in contact with one another. Opa Gus was such a gentle soul. He had an unwavering cheerful disposition, always smiling, in a good mood, and soft-spoken. It was only a handful of times that I got to experience that. I can't help but wish that I could have spent a lifetime with him. It is a strange phenomenon that I experience only with certain people.

I feel the need to express that I am not your average human being. People often refer to me as a sensitive or empathetic person because of my ability to understand and feel the emotions of others. That's not a title or a label, just an explanation of who I am. I was born as an energetic being in a human body. I can feel energy on many levels. As an empath, I have different needs than other humans. It took me a long time to discover and understand this. My needs include high frequency foods, the fresher the better. Solitude and quiet are also a must for me—as is water to submerge myself in, like a bath or pool. Not all sensitives are the same, but they do share many traits, such as a heightened sensitivity to energy and sensitivity to the emotions of others. Empaths often display supernatural abilities such as being able to read people's minds, sleeping dreams that later become reality, and predicting future events. Some special empaths see ghosts or spirits, or can move things with their minds. Seeing or doing these things is not something everyone is capable of. Each empath has their own set of abilities.

We went both to Disney World and Disneyland that summer. I remember vividly "feeling the magic" in both parks and being terrified of Mickey and Minnie. The "magic" is feeling other people's excitement, as I can feel most of the emotions of others, including both excitement and sadness. There is also a high concentration of dark energy from people suffering extreme anxiety and worse. People become anxious at those parks hundreds of times a day.

If you are sensitive to energy when you walk in, it can feel like butterflies in your stomach or solar plexus. That is how it manifests for me. I believe that all humans are unique and everything is not the same for everyone.

When I was three and four years old we once again came to the US for the summer and explored more places. The first time I saw the Grand Canyon, I was only three or four years old. I felt an inexplicable sense of belonging—like I had found my home. I would have the same sensations when I visited California, especially places like Lake Tahoe. I felt the same way when I visited the Arizona desert.

My parents were passionate about motorhomes and the freedom they provide to travel from one location to another. My father insisted on home-cooked meals and motorhomes allowed for that. We rarely spent more than two nights at any one location; most times, it was a single night. Their search for the perfect motorhome led them to purchase not one, but two; one in Spain and one in the U.S. They were way more than 'okay' financially. During my lifetime, my parents never had to work and continuously received money and prizes. They had a knack for winning raffles. They regularly won prizes, including a trip to Hawaii, cash, and other windfalls. They took the cash value rather than going to Hawaii as they preferred staying in a motorhome over a hotel.

You wouldn't know it from listening to the two of them. They were completely preoccupied with money, from who had it to how much everything costs. At every single meal, a rundown of the cost of the meal was done. It is all they ever talked about. Money tortured them, and guess what? They never ran out.

I vividly remember my parents asking me, at the tender age of four, if I would care for them in their later years. My love for them was so strong, so deep, that I didn't hesitate. "Of course, I will take care of you!"

My mom told me that they were serious. Without hesitation, I replied with every fiber of my soul that I was serious as well. As if to seal the deal, my mom suggested we shake on it. When we did, I felt tingles and shivers all up and down my spine. It was as if we had made a covenant. I knew right then and there that it was an unbreakable promise between us.

When I was four my neighbor Fabio introduced me to the concept of God. He said, "did you know we have another daddy? He lives in the sky. Anytime you are in trouble or lonely, you can talk to Him."

This completely resonated with me, like I always knew this to be true. I have a memory of drawing a picture on the floor of my father's office when I was four. The most beautiful energy showed up. It was what I now perceive as divine energy. It felt akin to being enveloped in a comforting warm blanket of the purest form of love known to mankind. My dad, who also had abilities, felt something happening and asked, "what is going on over there?"

I said, "I'm drawing a picture of my other daddy. He lives in the sky, and His name is God."

"Get over here." I walked over to my father's desk.

"There is no such thing as God. If there was a God, atrocities like concentration camps wouldn't happen. I never want to hear that nonsense again."

In my mind, I thought, "One day, I'll prove to you that God exists."

Shortly after that, my mom took me to my first concert. The performers were Albano and Romina Power. This concert was held at an amusement park called Tivoli in Benalmadena, Spain. When they sang the song, Felicita, I could feel what I now presume to be divine energy being exchanged. I am sure I got high on it. On my way home in the trunk of my mom's red Renault 5, I heard a voice asking me about the concert.

"It was incredible. The love between that couple was phenomenal."

"Yes, it was. We are here to tell you about your life," replied the familiar female voice.

"Hold on, if you know about my life when I am I going to meet my Albano?"

"At around the age your mother was when she had you, but we are not here to talk about that. We're here to talk about your life. You need to know that your life is going to be hard."

"Hard? I don't think so. I love life. I love being alive. This place is awesome," was my response.

"We are serious. You need to be prepared."

Although I was only four years old, I remember thinking to myself that I would cross that bridge when I got there. I was incredibly excited to be here and very skeptical. A year later, while I was walking around at the same theme park, I heard, "It's us again. We are back to tell you how serious we are that you are going to have a very hard life."

I replied, "So what?"

"We just need you to know."

CHAPTER 2

Joan of Arc

I n 1982, the town of Churriana, Spain was home to very rural folk. Churriana is a place that embodies the very essence of southern Spain. Nowadays, it's recognized as a district of Malaga, a major port city located on the southern coast of Spain. Even though we lived in Torremolinos, I was enrolled in Ciudad de Jaen, a public elementary school in Churriana. Since I had already completed kindergarten at my preschool, I started elementary in first grade. I found it difficult since most of my classmates had established friendships in kindergarten. I spoke little Spanish and definitely had a thick accent. The kids mercilessly teased me, which in today's times would be considered bullying. Even though my experience at that school was difficult, I was grateful for the friendship I had with Fabio. He was also a student there and was in my class.

Fabio's mom noticed the teasing in school because of my accent. For a few months, she gave me Spanish lessons after school. She wouldn't take no for an answer. Fabio's mother was the most wonderful mom you could ever imagine. She always added adventure to our time together, whether it was picking wildflowers, going on long hikes, or sharing entertaining stories. I secretly wished she were my mom.

We traveled around Spain, Portugal, and Southern France during my summer breaks when I was six, seven, and eight. Until my ninth year, everything was normal. The only metaphysical experiences I had were disembodied voices that kept asking me what I wanted to be when I grew up. I always answered, "Philosopher." However, I knew it wasn't practical because of the lack of earning potential. One day the nighttime voices came to me and said, "We are going to play a game today. We want to see if you can develop feelings for a rock."

"A rock? Get out of here... A rock, you guys are so silly," I laughed.

"Oh yeah? Try it," was their response. I went outside, picked up a rock, named it, and started petting it. To my surprise, I developed an affection for this non-living thing. When I got back to my room, I overheard the voices talking. "That was good. She can love anything."

I celebrated my ninth birthday in Pittsburg, Pennsylvania. We came to the U.S. for spring break 'plus'. The 'plus' was my mom convincing my teacher to allow me to miss school. She persuaded my teacher that travel was the highest form of education. In elementary school, I had all A's on my report card—even when I missed school.

∾

My uncle, Larry, and his wife, Elizabeth, met at a culinary institute in the Netherlands. Elizabeth was my mother's sister. Larry was originally from Jamaica, but had moved to Canada with his family. Uncle Larry was my favorite uncle. He taught me how to fish and use chopsticks.

We visited them previously in Denver during one of our summer trips.. They had also come to visit us in Spain.

Shortly after their visit, something happened that made my intuition and abilities to feel energy go away. They wouldn't return for quite some time. In the future, multiple mediums, who were strangers to one another, revealed that Larry (an energy worker) put a curse on me because of a negative spirit in his home.

Let me explain intuition. Intuition is your inner voice. Our inner voices can easily be influenced. If you are having repetitive negative thought patterns, I believe you have low frequency energies guiding you. You may not be aware that you are inviting these energies into your lives.

In order to communicate, or be influenced by higher frequency energies, you must be healthy. Eating clean and not indulging in addictions is part of that health. Addictions come in all kinds of shapes and packages. Some addicts believe they have their addiction under control because they are disciplined.

People can become addicted to activities such as gambling, shopping, video games, intimacy, and television; not just substances. Addictions are believed by some to create contracts with the dark side. Joy, adrenaline, and endorphins are some of the positive emotions produced by these activities. It's understandable why people tend to repeat things that bring them pleasure.

I take the inner voices seriously because they've shown me events before they have occurred. They've saved my life many times.

My ninth year was full of metaphysical events. While swimming in the pool one day, I noticed a few dead insects. I played a game where I pretended to bring them back to life by laying them on the stone border. I laid the insects on the warm stones and I said, "Abracadabra."

Suddenly, something came over me. I knew exactly what to do. I harnessed the power of the sun and moon, a concept that I had no prior knowledge of. While saying a prayer, I also poured love and affection into these beings. In that moment, I could feel a wave of divine energy surge through me. I felt overwhelming compassion for these creatures. I went back to swimming.

Twenty minutes later, I heard telepathically, "Go check on your bugs." When I went back, I was shocked to find they were all coming back to life. I said to myself, "Okay, these bugs were clearly waterlogged, and the sun dried them out. No way they came back to life."

The next day, I made another attempt. This time, I got some decaying ones and added them to the mix. I repeated the prayer, invoking the powers of the sun and moon, saying (once again) the magic word, "Abracadabra." I felt the divine energy coursing through me. Twenty minutes later I heard, "Your bugs are ready." To my astonishment, even the decaying bugs were coming back to life! It shocked me to realize that my eyes were not deceiving me. I couldn't wait to show Fabio.

The next day, I invited Fabio over for a swim. "Fabio, I'm going to perform a real-life magic trick for you. You see these bugs? We have some that are decaying as well, you see? Well, I'm going to bring them all back to life." After doing the ritual, we went for a swim. Twenty minutes later, "Your bugs are ready."

I was not expecting the reaction I got from Fabio. I expected him to find it extremely cool, but instead he reacted with a scream as if he were being killed in a horror film. In an effort to calm him down, I tried telling him that the sun had dried them out, but he continued to scream.

"What about the decaying ones? No way! No way!" That was the last thing Fabio said to me for the next two or three months.

A few months after this incident, I was in my third grade class studying Joan of Arc when the familiar female voice came on and said, "Let's play the breathing game I taught you." I felt divine energy around me. I reached the state where I left my body and found myself strolling in a medieval French town. It was loud and smelly. A young woman dressed in what seemed like battle or training gear led a horse through the town. I heard, "That is you, that is Joan of Arc." All I could think was, "Yeah, right!"

The divine energy stayed with me for the next two days after I came back to my body. That day, as I was leaving school, I thought to myself, "Wow, I have a wild imagination. With these kinds of skills, I know I'm going to be a writer when I grow up!"

I also thought, "If that was for real, that definitely explains the bugs coming back to life. Time will tell."

Around that same time my intuition told me I might move to the U.S. I received the idea telepathically. Part of the message I heard was, "It'd be easier for you there." That same year, while out at recess, a disembodied voice came to me—a clairaudient experience.

"When you grow up, you are going to have a daughter named Cielo, sky, and she is going to live in the sky." I thought to myself, "Does that mean I am going to have a child who dies?"

That winter, my sister Hazel and her husband bought a condo in Sierra Nevada, Spain, where our nearest ski resort was. We started spending many weekends and holidays there. Many people could sleep comfortably in the space. Hazel's husband was a gynecologist who had three children from a previous marriage: Maria, two years older than me, Isabel, who was my age, and Antonio, who was about five.

The first weekend we spent there, my sister took me skiing. Without knowing how to ski, she placed me on a lift and sent me to the top of the beginner's hill. My tears were flowing for a long time until a grumpy man came up to me and asked why I was crying.

"I don't know how to ski. My sister put me on this lift."

Begrudgingly, he said, "Take off your skis, we are walking down."

As I stood on that mountain, tears streaming down my face, I couldn't help but wonder what kind of world I was in—a world where nobody seemed to take notice of a sobbing child on a ski slope.

When I got down the mountain my sister was standing there with a beer and cigarette in hand laughing. She said, "stop exaggerating, it's not that bad."

Despite that painful experience, the nightclubs at the ski resort made it awesome, especially during a time in Spain when alcohol was available to anyone who could reach the counter. We were only allowed to go to the nightclub for a couple of hours. I remember ordering my first adult beverage at nine years old: Baileys with chocolate milk. Want to hear the sick part? They called it the children's drink. Our parents absolutely didn't care. My mom gave me permission to drink wine at the age of fifteen. Thank God, alcohol was never my thing. As soon as I could hold one, my parents allowed me to have a glass of Champagne on New Year's Eve.

One night, at the resort, we were late going home. Maria and I hitchhiked while we were walking back from the nightclub. A group of young men drove us up the hill to my sister's condo building. I couldn't believe we did that, but I didn't have a bad feeling, so I went along. The stairs leading to the condo building were about three flights long, straight up. We started our ascend. We were already ten minutes past our curfew. While climbing the stairs, I told Maria that I felt someone was following us. She agreed, but was too scared to look back.

"At some point, we have to turn around and take a look. I tell you what, on the count of three, we will both turn around to see. One, two, three!"

I laughed so hard that I literally peed my pants. There he was, coming up the stairs right behind us, a giant fluffy Saint Bernard. Animals are everything to me. I had an immediate sense that this one was following me. I didn't hesitate to give him a hug. He followed us into the building and came into the elevator with us. I had to pull him out of it. No one noticed we were late, thank God. Although we were usually punctual, the adventure we went on was worth being late.

One more strange thing happened on May 29, 1986. We were at my maternal grandfather's beachfront condo in Fuengirola, Spain. He had sold the one in Florida years earlier. My grandfather was known for using binoculars to watch beautiful girls at the beach from his condo. It was more than creepiness. He sincerely appreciated the female form. By being able to feel the emotions of others, I was able to understand what he was trying to say. During several summers in the U.S., my Opa Voormolen traveled with us. I would point out all the gorgeous girls to him during these trips. We would have a good laugh. He would often reassure me he only liked to look, that he would never touch any of these girls. I loved my Opa. We appreciated each other deeply.

My Aunt Alice and her husband were there for a visit from The Netherlands. She was the kindest of all my mother's sisters. I loved spending time with her. While waiting for someone to get ready, we witnessed hundreds of people flooding the street. That piqued our curiosity.

"Aunt Alice, do you think there could be a parade?"

"Do you want to go see?" she asked. A few moments later, we were out the door. Just as we were getting close to the massive crowd, we heard a loud boom. It was pretty clear what it was: an explosion. There was no parade.

No one was hurt in this bombing. We had a terrorist group in Spain called ETA. The Basques desired independence in the Basque country part of Spain. The consensus in the rest of Spain was that the Basque country needed the support of Spain to survive. ETA's modus operandi was to place a bomb, then call it in before it went off to evacuate potential victims. Things didn't always go according to plan when their bombs went off. ETA injured or killed many people. However, this was a clean bombing. A picnic gift basket was packed with explosives and left at The Hotel Las Palmeras, a five hundred and thirty thirty-five room hotel next door to my grandfather's building. Everyone got out in time.

The summer of my ninth year, we resumed our summer trips to the U.S. My sister Nicole had plans to start school as an exchange student in Wheeling, West Virginia, in order to distance herself from her father—who had managed to get out of jail. How, you may ask? My grandmother left my mother an inheritance while my mom was still legally married to the child molester. When my Oma passed, the molester was entitled to half the inheritance by law. To avoid any claim on the money, my mom struck a deal with his lawyers to drop the charges. So, he was released.

Because of his experience as a cop, my father knew how to get an illegal firearm in the US. During one of our summer trips to the US, we arrived in Texas with one goal in mind: find a gun show. My dad purchased a black-market revolver at the gun show. Once he had disassembled the revolver, he concealed its various parts in different compartments of his luggage, to smuggle them back to Spain undetected. In order to prevent Nicole's father from exercising his visitation rights with my sister, my father resorted to hiring a hitman. My mom was terrified that he would molest her as well, however, the night before the hit my mother canceled the plan because she got cold feet.

I clearly remember having my first psychic prediction when my mom told me they were going to sell our house. I knew with every fiber of my being that the good times were over. Live bands, flamenco dance troops, and guitar players were some common good times at the Van Den Bovenkamp parties hosted in that house. We had an outdoor bar that was only used for these extra special occasions. The joy and beautiful energy shared at these events was magical. My parents were amazing hosts, preparing all the food by themselves days in advance. There were few occasions where my dad would help my mom in the kitchen, that was one of them. He worked just as hard, if not harder.

Living in that home was absolutely the best time of my life, and I knew it when I lived there. Imagine knowing that, in advance. As a result, I didn't take a single moment for granted and appreciated everything. We had so many amazing memories of the most extraordinary

Christmas and holiday gatherings. The joy that was shared on that property was palpable to anyone who could feel energy, which I believed also allowed for the making of miracles. I believe love powers miracles. The pain of leaving that home is the only trauma I have never recovered from.

CHAPTER 3
Moving

A Chilean drug dealer bought our beloved house. He planned to renovate everything, add gold faucets, and bring his defense trained Dobermans onto the property—and all for $250,000. He paid all cash in American dollars. We had to move out right away.

My parents bought a townhouse in Playamar, a neighborhood near us that was closer to the beach. It was a new construction project of three-story townhomes. Ours was on a street called Benyamina. The bottom floor included a kitchen, dining room, living room, and half bath. The second story boasted three bedrooms. On the rooftop there was a terrace patio with a built-in outdoor kitchen. A fantastic place to have meals with neighbors and friends. All the floors were marble, even the stairs. I slipped and flew down those steps so many times.

There were a couple of great pluses to living there. The beach was within walking distance. Also within walking distance were shops, hair salons, bars, and more. We also had access to a basketball court at a nearby public school. The neighbors were awesome. Everyone on the street knew each other. It was not uncommon for neighbors to visit each other's homes for drinks, coffee, meals, and barbecues on the top terraces.

Two doors down, there was a family with two children, Alvaro and Virginia. Cerrado del Calderon was the name of the private school they attended. Even though the school was over an hour away in Malaga, it had a bus that picked students up in our neighborhood. My parent's friends also had their children studying in this school. During my elementary school years, my dad drove me to school in the mornings. I took the bus home. My parents had the idea to enroll me in this private school. My dad went along because it meant he didn't have to take me to school anymore in the mornings. I believe my mom wanted me to go there because her friend's kids went there. Although I had some reservations, the school's extensive sports and recreational programs, which included roller skating, volleyball, and swimming, sparked my interest. I started sixth grade there.

One of the reasons I also relented to going to this school is because my teacher at my public school was physically abusive, especially towards me. He would have been my educator for three more years. His wife had been my first through fifth grade teacher. In fifth grade, he came in to teach us math. He would often pick me up by my ears. He would pull my ears so hard that I feared they might tear. I have never told anyone, interestingly enough.

I would start my day earlier than in elementary school. At 7:30 a.m., I needed to be at the bus stop. My dad used to drop me off at 9 a.m. at my old school. I have always been nocturnal. I remember lying in bed for hours and hours, often listening to my parents go to bed. Playing with my teddy bear, Bobo, was how I entertained myself while lying down. Things would come to talk to me at night, usually around this time. No wonder I was terrified of the dark. I am no longer and that still is shocking to me. I believe starseeds, also know as empaths or sensitives, can function on less sleep. Getting up at 7 a.m. to rush to the bus stop by 7:30 a.m. was also getting to be too much for me. (Bobo still sleeps with me. If you had lived my life, you'd be sleeping with a teddy bear too.)

In Spain, there is always an ample lunch break for all schools, but my new school's lunch break was exceptionally long. The sports school, which produced Olympic athletes, had a four-hour lunch break that accommodated team practices, lunch, and siesta. Classes would resume at 4:30 p.m. and went through to 6:30. The bus dropped me off at home well past 7:30 p.m. I was home by five from my previous school.

During those lunch breaks, I would take part in every activity available to me. I played volleyball, took part in track, roller skated, and if there was a soccer game going on, I was on the team. All this activity left me exhausted. By the time I came home and sat down to do homework, I couldn't concentrate. My grades were slipping. I barely passed sixth grade. As a starseed child, my favorite pastime was gazing at the sky for hours on end. My desk was facing a window. I would lose myself in the beauty of the Andalusian sky for hours. It is a different blue than other parts of the world. It is a deep blue that I couldn't get enough of. Apparently, looking at the sky for hours is a starseed child trait.

After my sister, Nicole, went to the U.S. as an exchange student, she absolutely fell in love with the country. She did both her junior and senior year in Wheeling, West Virginia. There she met a boy named Thomas. They fell in love and got married.

My sister was studying aerospace engineering at the University of Florida during my seventh grade when random murders occurred. Thomas was enlisted in the Navy. He went on a six-month tour in the Mediterranean. When he stopped in our hometown, my parents picked him up. It was so weird seeing him there, in Spain. I also heard, "He is cheating on your sister. Do you feel all those female energies?" The murders became a sign for my parents to move to the U.S., as they were already considering the idea.

After sitting me down, they said, "Ultimately, it's up to you." My intuition had already told me several times, suggesting that a move to the U.S. was a good idea. They emphasized that schooling would be so much easier there. Without hesitation, I agreed with their suggestion, as I was struggling with every subject except electives and science.

Seventh grade was kicking my butt. Starseed children often have ADHD and tire easily.

After having seen some of my prayers answered, I promised to recite ten Lord's Prayers and twenty Hail Mary every night until the end of seventh grade. I was praying for a miracle from God to help me pass.

When my science teacher gave me my report card on the last day of seventh grade, I was devastated. I had four or five F's on my report card.

Tears started flowing when I thought about all the praying. My science teacher had a wonderful energy about him, almost divine. He came over and asked what was wrong. I said, "We are moving to the U.S. in two days. I have F's on my report card, and summer school is not an option!"

"Give me that." My science teacher took my report card and disappeared. His absence was long enough that the classrooms closed, which led me to wait for him at the school's study hall. We had a classroom that was centrally located that was turned into a study hall where you could study any time of day. I sat there for what felt like forever.

When my teacher finally returned, he said, "I have good news and bad news. I got all your grades changed except for math. That teacher wouldn't budge."

I started crying again, "I absolutely cannot go to summer school."

As this was happening, my math teacher walked past the study hall. My science teacher grabbed my report card and vehemently accosted the other teacher in the hallway. I saw them arguing, my math teacher shaking his head. Finally, I saw my math teacher throwing his hands up in the air and relenting, signing my report card!

As I was walking out of the school, divine energy came over me. I heard telepathically, "This doesn't happen to normal people."

I thought to myself, *it sure doesn't*. Just as I had prayed for, my grades had been changed. My prayers came true so often that I absolutely, unequivocally, became scared to pray and would go many, many years without praying.

In order to avoid making my dad angry, I kept quiet about my prayers around my parents. Once I wrote some prayers in the margin of my notebook. My sister Hazel saw them, grabbed my notebook, and ran to show my dad. My embarrassment and shame were so overwhelming that I could no longer bring myself to pray. It felt like I was doing something wrong. I realize now that she was under the influence of unseen things that led her to do that to keep me from praying. I never blamed her.

A few summers before, my parents purchased a house in the U.S. for my sister Nicole, with the understanding that we would live there during the summer months. Now, we were going to live there full time with her and her husband. This home was in Jacksonville, Florida. Nicole and her husband had moved there after he got stationed there with the Navy. It was a three-bedroom, one story, new construction home in a neighborhood where most homes looked the same. I couldn't help but notice how thin the walls were in our American home. Even behind closed doors, you could hear everyone's conversations.

We didn't know that my sister was in an abusive relationship. She would deny it and come up with excuses. One day he was laying into her again in the bathroom. I confronted him. Despite my sister's objections, my unwavering bravery and intolerance for injustices compelled me to take action. Thomas picked me up like I weighed nothing and threw me across the hallway against the wall of the foyer. I was twelve. This must have scared him because there was no more abuse for a while.

The energy in Florida is weird. There is so much metaphysical stuff going on in that state. It's just a weird place. My mother used to claim that there was something strange in the earth. I now suspect that she may have sensed what I perceive to be Native American curses.

My mom believed in psychics. She trusted a psychic who lived in a remote village in Spain. The psychic was not very well known. Over the years, this psychic provided her with extremely accurate advice. She told my sister Nicole that she would marry a man in the military and have two children. Nicole laughed at this, as she already knew she couldn't have children. But that is exactly what would transpire for Nicole. Her husband just retired from the military, and she has two kids. The psychic told my mom she had a gifted child, and mom said to me, "It has to be Hazel." I laughed and thought to myself, "I know exactly who that is." My mother was so convinced it was Hazel that I decided not to say anything. It was very clear to everyone that my sister Hazel was my mom's favorite. I absolutely didn't mind. They had a bond that transcended this world. I could feel it.

Around the age of twelve, we were camping in Saint Augustine, Florida, as we did often. I spent many spring breaks, summer breaks, and weekends at the Bryn Mawr Ocean Resort. While we were on a trip, my parents, who consumed copious amounts of alcohol every evening, confronted me at the back of the motorhome. "You are jealous of your sister Hazel." I had no idea where that came from.

"What?" I asked, perplexed.

"You are jealous of your sister Hazel. That is why the two of you don't get along." My sister and I didn't get along because I rubbed her the wrong way. She didn't like my energy or light.

"Mom, Dad, I swear, I am not the least bit jealous of Hazel."

"You are lying," accused my dad, who usually always had my back. I sensed that something was wrong and quickly got up, saying, "I swear I'm not jealous of Hazel. I don't know what else to do to convince you."

Walking is one of my favorite ways to clear my head, so I went for a long walk around the campground. When I returned, it was like nothing had ever happened.

My parents quickly realized that the responsibilities of rearing a child interfered with their carefree, retired lifestyle. I think I was five the first time they floated the idea of a boarding school. Apparently, I hadn't shown enough disgust because, about eighteen months later, my dad approached me with some brochures from these boarding schools. Thank God my father could feel the emotions of others because panic came over me. My parents were my everything. There was no way I wanted to be without them. I still don't, but alas, I don't have a choice now. When my dad sensed my panic, the discussion was over and it was never, ever brought up again. They chose my sister Hazel as my care-taker when they had to travel instead. After my sister Nicole became an exchange student, my parents would travel to the U.S. for six to eight weeks every winter. I would stay with Hazel, which only had one plus: skiing almost every weekend. Eventually, I learned how to ski and became good at it. I always wanted to be the fastest kid on the moun-tain, and telepathically I would hear, "You will not always feel the need to be the fastest person on the mountain."

When I was eighteen, I went skiing in Snowshoe, West Virginia. I remember hearing, "This is your last skiing experience for a very long time."

During a weekend, my sister and her husband invited a doctor from Switzerland to join us. I heard, "Pay attention, this will be you some-day." Although he was in his forties, the man used to be an avid skier before he turned eighteen. He hadn't skied since then. So, after his first few runs, I asked him, "How was it?"

"Like riding a bicycle," was his response, much to my relief. I wouldn't ski again until I was forty-four. The most shocking part... I didn't have to be the fastest person on the mountain! I now realize that drive stemmed out of insecurities.

~

After my incident with Thomas, Nicole started looking for a house of their own. My parents would help with the down payment. As a military couple, they qualified easily for a loan. After Nicole and Thomas moved out, my parents would leave me home alone. This started at twelve, sometimes for weeks at a time—once for six weeks. When I was a child, I displayed a high level of maturity, and was incredibly independent. This turned out to be a good thing, as my parents were definitely hands off in their parenting style. I only threw one party, during my senior prom. They left me home alone for that, too.

My parent's hands-off parenting style led me to going to theme parks like the Magic Kingdom by myself. Solitude has never been a problem for me. The night before my theme park adventure, I could feel a sense of divine energy surrounding me. I initially thought it was just the butterflies that I felt from the excitement. After reflecting on my experiences in those parks, I have come to the belief that it was divine beings shielding me from the dark energies and negative people present in those areas. In 2019, while at the park, I witnessed a massive energy cleaning for God. I believe the angels produced a blackout, or several blackouts, to clear out the energy. The park felt so good afterward; it was like being in contact with the divine.

From the age of ten, I was extremely independent and self-sufficient. I used to have my dad drop me off at a bus stop as early as five in the morning, where I would embark on a three-hour bus journey to the ski resort by myself. There I would spend the entire day skiing. On those mountains were some of my favorite memories. Me, myself, and snow. I loved skiing so much that I often didn't even take a lunch break or have anything to drink, skiing for eight or nine hours straight.

CHAPTER 4

Mr. Gere

The summer of seventh grade, my intuition telepathically told me that all fours were going to come out in the lottery. Four, fourteen, twenty-four, thirty-four, and forty-four. When I told my mom to play some lotto numbers that I came up with, she was pleased to do it. I revealed all the numbers to her except forty-four, because reciting all those fours made me feel silly. To be honest, I believed it to be a metaphysical joke. Imagine my surprise when my mom comes home and says she got four numbers in the lottery, the ones I gave her. I asked if forty-four was one of the numbers that was called and she said, "Yes, it was."

I then asked myself why my mother wasn't more impressed. I was shown that something was influencing her not to notice, as what truly had transpired was a miracle—but she wasn't meant to know. This nonsense shocked me to some extent. Was I supposed to believe that I am the reincarnation of Joan of Arc, that I can bring insects back to life, and predict winning lottery numbers? Insert eye roll.

School in the U.S. was a surreal experience. Children were different. Geography and world events were not their strong suits. The Berlin wall had just come down. These kids had no idea what I was talking about. "Do they speak Spanish in Spain?" was a question that was frequently asked. Then there were some other issues, like how I dressed differently. The style when I left Spain was bell bottoms and polo shirts. Spain's style in the late 80s and early 90s was eclectic, and everyone wore the same things. Once, it became all the rage to wear yellow Panama Jack boots. Half the city was walking around in those. It was an incredible sight to see. And of course, I spoke English with an accent. They teased me relentlessly about that. That didn't keep me from loving bell bottoms any less.

The energy and smell of school buildings in the U.S. were quite odd to me. This school, Thomas Jefferson Middle School, was no exception. These buildings felt like they were void of love to me. It felt almost like you were in an artificial environment. However, just like I was promised by the things that talk to me, school was much easier in the U.S. Not only was it easier, but the teachers actually taught. Classroom participation was encouraged. At my last school, if you asked a question, you were talked down to, thus discouraging any questions. While opinions on the American school system vary, I found it more educational than the system in Spain. During my eighth-grade year there, I experienced racism for the first time.

Under the circumstances that I grew up, I never knew of racism. People in my school admired the two black young men who studied there. We were all fans of Michael Jordan and Michael Jackson. We thought black people were the coolest. At this school, black and white children barely acknowledged each other. I felt like I was in the Twilight Zone. It absolutely shocks me that people can't see each other as equals.

Yahweh (God) docs.

The only hiccup in my eighth-grade experience was being bullied, particularly by a neighboring girl, but it didn't affect me much.

I spent the summer of my fourteenth year with my sister, Hazel, at her house back in Spain. Her daughter, Maria, now sixteen, was allowed to go to nightclubs pretty much every night during the summer. I was just enough of a pain in my sister's rear that I talked her into letting me tag along with Maria. What a summer we had! Starting the day around eleven or twelve, we headed to the beach, enjoyed Spanish steak hoagies for lunch, and took a siesta on the sand. After dinner, which was around nine, we would get ready for the nightclub. Usually, a few girls would get together and we would do each other's hair. We didn't wear makeup. We dressed up like we were heading for the club, wearing miniskirts and crop tops, showing off our beautiful figures.

Everyone would order the same drink. We drinking screwdrivers because in those days in Spain, no one cared how old you were. There were many nights I didn't drink, though. I got high on the music, the energy, and the friendship I had with these girls.

What a great time of my life. When I came back to the U.S., I missed my homeland so terribly, I would cry often. But this was nothing new. My first love was my home, the beaches, the hills, the people, the food, the sky—I can go on and on.

I started high school at N.B. Forest High School, a school named after the founder of the KKK. I had an encyclopedia in my room and looked it up. When I told kids at school, no one believed me. I thought to myself, does everything in my life need to be so freaking weird?

Following a series of episodes by NPR that highlighted the problematic nature of a school named after the founder of the KKK, they officially renamed the institution West Side High.

On the first day of school, while I was sitting in my homeroom, I heard telepathically, "We know four years is a long time; and it will feel like a very long time. But in the scope of your life, it will be a blip." I could feel divine energy surging through me. At that moment, I knew I would make it through.

Being an ambivert, I can be very social in social situations. However, my preference lies in being alone and enjoying the quiet. High school was not for me. Too many people, those awful fluorescent lights, and loud teenagers. I hated it. A few months into it, I decided I was going to become part of the popular kids, mostly because I was bored and needed a challenge. I started wearing makeup and really cool outfits. One of the unspoken rules that cool girls followed at that school was to never wear the same outfit twice. I made sure to mix and match my wardrobe to avoid repeating an outfit as much as possible. I would spend over an hour every morning doing my makeup and hair, a habit I kept up all four years. Although I am no longer trying to be popular, I still wear makeup because I believe that presenting your best self is a way of showing kindness to others. I personally enjoy when people look their best, so I try to do the same.

I joined the swim team to stay in shape. My weight was a bit of an obsession, mostly because of my mom's comments every time I gained a pound. Even though my mom was overweight and had been her whole life, she always made comments about other people's weight. I only gained my mother's approval when I would lose weight.

Shortly after school started, a sophomore named Kevin started showing interest in me. We would walk to class together, sometimes holding hands. We may have kissed a few times. Our phone conversations would last for hours. He was on the track and field team. They had made it to the state championships. The night before the state meet, he had stayed up all night with his grandmother as she was passing away. As a result, he had missed the state championship. He was part of the relay team. This made him feel like he had let everyone down, and he had also recently lost a sister to overdose. While talking on the phone with him trying to console him, my sister, Nicole, kept calling, saying she needed to talk to my mom. I begged her. I told her I was on a very important phone call. She threatened to come over and tell my mother that I refused to let her speak to her, which made me hang up.

The next day, someone from school called me and said, "Did you hear what happened to Kevin? He committed suicide yesterday."

"What? At what time did this happen?" I remember it being less than two hours since I got off the phone with him. I was so disappointed that my sister didn't trust my instincts. This was when I was introduced to valium. (I had access because my mom, who believed everything every doctor ever told her, loved pills.) Shopping for the funeral outfit the next day felt surreal. My first boyfriend had committed suicide. Why was my life always so dramatic?

I made a Mexican friend named Nora. Nora was one of the popular kids. She was one of the prettiest girls I had ever seen. Nora was also friends with some cool kids at our neighboring school, Orange Park High School. They were between a year and four years older than us. They either had cars or access to cars. That spring break, we all started hanging out together. Dustin was the youngest of the group. We immediately bonded. He became my boyfriend a few weeks before my fifteenth birthday.

Since his family was from Ecuador, he could speak Spanish. Spanish is my best language. I learned English through my various trips to the U.S., and my mother's determination. When I was a child, we had a VHS system. We rented movies for this system at the local video club, like a Blockbuster Video. Both of my parents spoke English perfectly, as it is something many Dutch children are taught from a young age. The best movie selection was at the English video club in town. They decided we would only rent English movies. When I protested, my mother insisted that I needed to learn English. I remember watching Superwoman and not understanding a single word. Telepathically, a few days later, I would hear, "It is very important for you to hear and learn English. Spanish is also an important language for your journey."

I, of course, would give them the eye roll. When we first moved to the U.S., I still didn't consider myself able to speak the language. I was fluent in six weeks. The transformation was insane, how quickly I picked up everything. Since then, I have tried learning different languages and have observed the same phenomenon.

Telling my parents about my first serious boyfriend was a nerve-wracking experience. Much to my surprise, they were okay with it. I confided in my dad, who was a romantic at heart in order to gain my mother's approval. I'm not sure how, but he convinced her. Dustin wore his pants low. It drove my mom crazy.

"Cristina, can't you tell him to pull up his pants?"

"Lol, Mom, no, it's what is in style," I laughed.

We had been dating for a few months when a planned trip to Spain came up. Once we were airborne, a party broke out in the back of the airplane with drinks being passed around, including vodka that I took a few sips of. I couldn't resist. How often does a fifteen-year-old get to drink vodka at an impromptu airplane party? So, yes, I had that experience for the Universe. Too bad smart phones weren't a thing yet because it was a sight to be seen. All the passengers were in the back of the airplane, "the smoking section."

The usual going to the beach, partying all night, and repeat, was just amazing. Again, one of the best summers of my life. It was devastating to leave. To this day, I cry every single time I think of my home, my first love. I truly fell in love with the place the way you would with a star-crossed lover. Knowing that I would never again return to Spain for the summer intensified my pain ten fold. Because she had a month left of her summer break, Maria came back with me to the U.S. Dustin was the first person Maria wanted to see upon our return. I thought Dustin's neck had gotten bruised while playing basketball. Maria came up to me and said, "Are you seriously that naïve? That is not a bruise. It's a hickey."

The realization hit that Dustin had been unfaithful. The pain that set in was beyond anything I had previously experienced. I had already received physical beatings from a wide range of folks. (People would become violent towards me with no justification, solely because the dark side influences them.) This pain was beyond anything physical I had ever experienced. This pain also made me vow to myself that I would never be anyone's "other woman." I could never inflict this kind of pain on any female.

I had received beatings from my sisters and from schoolmates. One in particular did hurt my self-esteem and left a mark. My neighborhood friends were three boys, Fabio, Alex, and Manuel. Over the course of two consecutive weeks, they made it their mission to come together and physically assault me. I remember trying not to puke from the impact of their punches on my stomach. It was a devastating realization that the people who were supposed to be my friends could do something like that. As a result, I learned how to fight. When they made their third attempt, I felt a sudden surge of confidence, and my inner Bruce Lee emerged. Despite never having taken martial arts, I fought with the precision and skill of a black belt karate master. Suddenly the boys suggested, "Why don't we play a different game...." Little did I know, those skills would make an appearance again later on in my life.

Of course, I broke things off with Dustin. At around the same time, my mother became drunk and began calling me a whore. I believed her. A world where mothers call their daughters whores was not a world I wanted to be in. That night, I had the brilliant idea to end my life. I went into the bathroom where I started downing every pill in sight. I took a variety of medicines, including pills like Advil, Tylenol, and some European medications my mom had brought over. One bottle alone had eighty pills and was almost full. When I was done, I went to bed and prayed with all my will I would not wake up. I said to myself, "If I wake up from this one, it is truly God's will for me to be here."

It took me aback when I woke up. Perhaps I was genuinely on a divine mission, I thought to myself. The day I woke up, we were leaving to go on a trip with our motorhome. I believe we were going to Tennessee to visit Opryland. The trip took several days. There was only one issue with my suicide attempt. I woke up blind. I told Maria what was going on and made her swear to keep it a secret. She would one day become a doctor. She definitely got to practice her bedside manner during those three days. I remained blind. I slept all day. Something supernatural seemed to be healing me. My parents only saw me at break-fast and dinner. I was so relieved my parents didn't realize what was happening. Not hurting my parents was a priority for me, though you could not tell by my suicide attempt.

On the third day, as soon as I opened my eyes, I found myself back to normal. My mind felt slightly overwhelmed by the experience. During that trip, I had a dream that felt very realistic. In my dream, Dustin met a girl with long black hair extending past her tushy. In the dream, he got her pregnant shortly after meeting her, which caused the end of our relationship. Because of the realistic nature of this dream, I felt compelled to call Dustin from a payphone. He said he missed me and loved me. He claimed he had no intention of encountering a girl with long black hair. We patched things up over the phone. I was so relieved. Even though I wasn't in love with Dustin, I believed I was because I didn't clearly understand what that emotion was supposed to feel like. I love everyone. Love that's worth climbing Mount Everest for is something I've only experienced once in my life.

In September, Maria went home. We planned for me to visit during winter break. I spent my Christmas break skiing in Spain. I would fly by myself often. This actually started when I was nine or ten. My parents often liked to take road trips to the Netherlands. They would drive there over the course of two days. In the beginning, my mom still smoked a lot during our car trips. The smoke made me nauseous. We had to stop every few hours for me to throw up. After a few trips like these, they decided I would fly by myself to Holland. Someone would come get me at the Schiphol Airport in Amsterdam. We had a lot of family in the

Netherlands. I had aunts and uncles, siblings from my father's previous relationships, and my parents still had lots of friends there.

Just a few months prior to my winter trip, DC10 airplanes were having hydraulic systems issues. Some had crashed. I always flew the same route, Jacksonville to Miami, Miami to Madrid, Madrid to Malaga, and the reverse on the way back. Although my flight to Madrid was fine on the return trip, I encountered a delay of eight hours when I arrived at the Madrid Airport. The DC10 we were supposed to board was having technical difficulties. Because of the circumstances, Iberia graciously treated us to a meal at the airport's cafeteria. Whenever I traveled with Iberia Airlines, I always found their service exceptional. The flight attendants were like typical Spanish moms, they were always nurturing and truly concerned. The airline was always great at providing delicious meals to their passengers. As soon as I boarded an Iberia airline, I would immediately start feeling at home.

Since I was traveling alone, I sat by myself in the cafeteria, trying to enjoy my meal. By the age of fifteen, I had dozens of solo trips under my belt. A man approached my table. He was Richard Gere's doppelgänger, "Me puedo sentar?" *Can I sit down?*

"Claro." *Of course.*

It turns out this Richard Gere was a reporter for a well-known Latin American television chain. He showed me his different passports and all the stamps from different countries. He recounted tales of near bombings, and he mentioned he had covered many wars. Afterward, I agreed to go for a walk around the airport. We had some time to kill. While we were walking, I felt divine energy come over me. I now believe it was angels protecting me. Mr. Gere and I hit it off. Many more hours went by before we could board our DC10. He immediately started planning for us to sit together. He found a way. We had been in the air for roughly an hour and forty-five minutes when the pilot made an announcement over the intercom stating that we would be returning to Madrid because of an issue with the hydraulic systems. I grabbed the reporter's hand.

"This is the issue that has made all those DC10s crash." I was slightly frightened. I don't frighten easily. I said a Lord's Prayer. A few minutes later, the pilot came on.

"The problem seems to have resolved itself on its own, and we are continuing on to Miami."

So yes, just in case I didn't arrive alive, me and Gere started making out. I managed to disembark the airplane a virgin...barely.

I knew I was in trouble. I knew it was not natural to lust after a fifteen-year-old, magical as she may be. Yahweh had it all figured out. We had just landed when customs officers came on board the plane to inform us that there was a minor named Cristina Bovenkamp traveling with us—and to "please come forward." Mercy! Mr. Gere immediately acted as if he didn't know who I was. Due to the eight-hour delay, I had to spend the night at a customs office at the Miami Airport, sitting uncomfortably in a chair, as there were no available flights until morning to Jacksonville. Better than spending the night with Mr. Gere. Thank you angels.

CHAPTER 5

You are About to Marry a Demon

In the spring after my sixteenth birthday, my saga with my bully came to blows. We had the same homeroom that year. One day after class, she began to bully me in the hallway. When I was walking away, she hit me on the back. I turned around and watched her wagging her finger in my face as she was talking smack. I once again turned around and left. As I was leaving, my body unexpectedly pivoted around all on its own. Though my first instinct was flight, my natural instinct is fight as I was about to find out.

What happened next was like something out of a movie as I fought her Bruce Lee style. I was once again fighting like a skilled martial artist. She landed one punch on my eyebrow as I simultaneously broke her nose. After she landed her punch, time slowed down to a crawl; I was able to calculate every move effortlessly. We continued to battle until I grabbed her by the shoulders and slammed her against the wall. That finally got her to stop.

Strangely, no teachers showed up. I picked up my backpack and started walking to my math class. As I was walking my eye started twitching. When I wiped, I had blood on my hand. I also saw blood all over my dress; I realized I couldn't go to class. Her nose had exploded all over my dress. I realized I had to go to the principal's office. When I

39

arrived at the principal's office, the vice-principal informed me she absolutely had to call my parents. I was terrified. It was the first time I had ever been in trouble. I made a futile attempt to get her to not call my parents. My parents were older. I certainly never wanted to give them any grief.

My mom was aware of my bully, as she often called our landline phone to harass me. I really rub some folks the wrong way and when that happens, sometimes they become fixated. To my shock, surprise and delight, my mom's first words out of her mouth after she arrived were, "Did you get her good?" I had never loved my mom more than I did at that moment. On the way home, she said, "Don't worry about your suspension. We're taking advantage of our time off to visit the theme parks in Orlando."

Dustin and I were on and off. We didn't go to the same school, and we only saw each other on the weekends. When I was fifteen, my parents allowed me to spend weekends at Dustin's house.

Dustin's parents were workers in a factory. They worked long hours. They were also hands off and didn't seem to care who spent the night. I started spending the weekends at Dustin's house in his bed.

My parents bought me my first car six months before my sixteenth birthday because they were eager for me to drive. The day before I turned sixteen, I started work at our local Taco Bell. I enjoyed the fast-paced environment. Although my favorite role was working the line, I was always assigned to the front or the drive-thru as a cashier. Even though my parents bought my car, I took care of the insurance, maintenance, and gas, as well as buying all my own clothes. I was so happy to be able to contribute.

To start pre-calculus in the fall, I enrolled in a summer school math credit. That summer, I studied trigonometry. It was the absolute worst summer of my life. I vowed to never repeat that mistake. I really disliked school. But like a good soldier, I did my part. That class also completed all of my prerequisite math credits, and I actually decided no more math. Ugh. During those math classes, I had a feeling that they would never be useful to me. I turned out to be correct. I never used those skills.

Dustin and I broke up again after that summer. This was a longer than usual break up. I had not heard from him for two weeks. I went to his house to see if we could reconcile. When I got there, Dustin was just arriving. When the passenger door opened, I was in severe and utter shock. The girl in my dream, the one with long black hair past her butt, appeared before me. I somehow managed to keep my composure. Knowing already that she was pregnant, I decided to just make some polite small talk. I knew I had to get out of there as soon as possible because I would never get involved in a situation like that. That was my first dream that had ever become a reality. I was astonished.

I was working with a Latin girl, and we were talking in Spanish when a really good-looking guy came in. "Hey, can you say something in Spanish?" This was a common question from an American male. I chuckled and asked my coworker in Spanish about the size of his "peesh." Surprisingly, this blonde, blue-eyed Jean-Claude Van Damme doppelgänger responded flawlessly in Castilian Spanish. I now understood how people felt when they met me. It was like the Twilight Zone. Here was this all-American boy, a head turner, speaking my native language.

All at once, I felt embarrassed, delighted, and stunned. We made some very polite small talk after that. I was truly only joking. As attractive as he was, he wasn't my type, but it was fun talking to a kid from Spain. His mother was from the Canary Islands. My family had its own Canary Islands connection. That is where my mom had started her business, which she later sold to my uncle, one of her sisters' husbands. Things went very well for him in the Canary Islands after that. My mom would often say to me, "I'd rather have you than all the money in the world," and she meant it.

His name was Daniel. He was born in Rota, Spain, just a few hours from where I was born, in the same province—Andalucia. When you come from that province, you have an ingrained provincial pride. All Andalusians are your neighbors, friends. Being born there is definitely one of the top experiences of my life. He was born on a Navy base and his father's current deployment was in Jacksonville, Florida. His parents bought a house a few months before in Orange Park, a town adjoining

Jacksonville. Daniel mentioned joining the National Guard Reserves and heading to boot camp.

A few months went by. I didn't give our encounter another thought. He came in one day with the appearance of a bodybuilder. When all the girls at Taco Bell were swooning over him, I couldn't resist approaching him. The whole thing felt off. After walking over to his table, I asked him if he would like to go out to the movies later that evening. Even though he was extremely charming, a go-getter and assertive, he was emotionless, so it was effortless to be near him. When we went to the movies, I became intrigued by this person whose emotions I couldn't feel. We started dating, and when he introduced me to his mom, Juana, the strangest thing happened. I felt like I knew her my whole life. Now I realize we had a past life connection. She, too, has supernatural abilities, telekinesis. She has made things levitate before.

Juana was one of twelve siblings and grew up very poor in the Canary Islands. She was exquisite, with black hair, black eyes, and petite. Juana would later share a story with me that one day she had a dream while they were living at this trailer park. In the dream, she saw a Ouija board in a neighbor's trailer. When she woke up, she walked over there out of curiosity to see if there was indeed a Ouija board over there. Through a window she saw the Ouija board. To her surprise, the door was wide open. It was inviting her to grab it, so she did. She said that the moment she brought the Ouija board into her house the energy in her home changed. She felt it. She told the boys, Daniel and his brother, not to touch the board. The boys didn't listen and played with it. After a few days, she couldn't stand the energy anymore and threw it away. Much to her surprise, the Ouija board was back where she left it the next day. She questioned the boys, "which one of you took it out of the trash?" They denied it. She didn't believe them. On the next garbage day, she put it out again and once again it showed up the following day. The kids swore up and down that they didn't bring it back in. After three attempts, she drove it away from the house to dispose of it elsewhere. Guess what showed up again at her house?

Juana phoned a friend. "I know you're interested in the paranormal. A Ouija board keeps reappearing at my home, despite my attempts to get rid of it. I've thrown it in the trash and even driven it far away, but it keeps coming back."

"Oh, that is a spelled Ouija board. Give it away," was the answer she got. "Place it somewhere. If someone takes it, you are rid of it." The next day she placed it by the kid's school bus stop and by the afternoon it was gone, not to return.

Juana and Albert met in Rota, Spain. I believe neither spoke each other's language when they got married. Albert was in the Navy his whole life. They had two sons, Daniel and Larry. The couple was separated for many years, during which Juana went back to Spain with her boys. Eventually, they would reconcile and move back with Albert in Orange Park, Florida.

Daniel had just returned from boot camp. He was twenty years old. Although he had two jobs, his main occupation was working as a waiter at the Olive Garden. He was also a part-time DJ, which was very attractive to a teenage girl who absolutely adored music. Six months after we started dating, he proposed to me unexpectedly. Being completely clueless about setting boundaries, I said yes. How many other chances would I get to marry a good-looking guy from my home country? I swear girls need a realistic class on how love works, seriously. Do you know how many people wind up in the wrong relationship because they have seen too many Hollywood movies?

I said yes. I agreed to marry a man I was not attracted to, and most definitely was not in love with, because we liked the same food and music. Solid marriage foundation, don't you think?

I was in the U.S. under a student visa that would expire when I graduated high school. I found this out after I had already said yes to his marriage proposal. We decided that after my high school graduation that we would get married. My parents paid for the wedding, set to happen on July 8th, 1995.

Right after graduation, Richard deployed for his summer tour with the National Guard Reserves. When he came back I started experiencing nausea. I thought it was pre-wedding jitters. My bust had also mysteriously tripled in size. I took a pregnancy test. It was in a Burger King bathroom that I found out I was going to be a mom. I had no doubts about having this child. Daniel and I kept the news a secret until after

43

the wedding since his mother had called us over to have a talk after he came back from his deployment. At first, his parents had no objections to our marriage and were fully supportive. Their big announcement was that Juana and Albert were going to adopt another child because Juana felt she was losing her son. I didn't know what to say. Congratulations? Aren't you a little old to be adopting children?

I think what came out was something like 'go for it.' That was not the reaction she was hoping for. I don't know. Maybe she had envisioned her son saying, "Oh mom, please don't replace me, I won't marry her." My mother-in-law put on a white dress to attend our wedding.

That was just the beginning.

The wedding planning kept me busy that summer. I found the most beautiful dress on a clearance rack. It had tiny pink roses sewn into it, and I knew instantly when I saw it that it was the one. There was divine energy in that dress. Now, looking back, I know the angels made those arrangements. It was a little big at the waist. The shop lady said she could have it taken in with no issues and to come back two weeks before the wedding. When I came back two weeks prior, the dress fit me perfectly. My mom would later confess that was the first time she suspected I was pregnant.

The wedding was being held at the Orange Park Women's Club, followed by a catered reception. My in-laws invited close to two hundred strangers, neighbors. There were only a handful of people I knew at my wedding. It was a beautiful setting. My mom insisted on fresh flowers, and it was charming.

While standing and waiting for my father to join me at the top of the aisle, I had my first clairaudient experience as an adult. Clairaudience is when you hear a disembodied voice. It's like someone is talking to you, but there is no one there.

I heard, "You are about to marry a demon."

"What?" I exclaimed. The idea of demons, angels, or anything else of the sort was completely foreign to me since I didn't believe in them. Telepathically, I then heard, "He is part of your path, all will be well."

Although all I had seen was a charming, hard-working young man, I could feel this was a real warning. When I walked towards him and saw him smile, I knew. I had a horrible feeling in my midsection. But at that moment, you think you are delusional because it's irrational. I went through with the wedding mostly to please my parents. I didn't think I would have their support if I changed my mind at the altar. Plus, they had shelled out a lot of money for this shindig. Oh, and did I mention I was pregnant? I was in a tough spot. I got my first glimpse of the demon a few hours later on our wedding night.

CHAPTER 6
We Need to Talk

Because we had little money, our honeymoon was just a couple of nights at an oceanside hotel in Saint Augustine, Florida. Saint Augustine was the only place in Florida where I had found good energy. Saint Augustine was a short drive from our home.

I took up body surfing in my teenage years while dating a boy who surfed. One day I woke up and heard, "Today is the last day you will go surfing." I rolled my eyes. I never trusted or believed these things, but as I would find out later in life, those messages were very accurate. The plan was to skip school and go surfing in Saint Augustine. We got there after 8 a.m., and we couldn't believe our eyes when we arrived. The ocean was like a lake, but there were six to eight-foot waves. On a good day, we got two to three feet. During the initial four hours of our surfing excursion, we had the entire beach to ourselves. We took full advantage of the opportunity by surfing until we were completely exhausted. We laid down on the sand for twenty minutes, then we would go right back in.

It was the most incredible experience. Later on, we stopped in at the local surf shop to get some wax. The guys at the shop were beside themselves. They had never seen anything like it. According to the man who lived there for twenty years, the day was unlike any other he ever witnessed before. Raised by miracles. I find it humbling that God made my last surfing experience so special.

Daniel and I checked into our hotel at 10 p.m. After we checked in, I went to change into something a little more comfortable, if you will—some lingerie. It didn't take very long, but when I came out of the bathroom, my husband was gone. My husband's absence perplexed me. I sat there and waited. An hour went by. Now I was thinking something had happened to him. I got dressed and went looking for him. I went to the pool. There was no sign that anyone had been there. I couldn't find him. I started going toward the beach. As I approached the sand, a sinister feeling came over me, so I turned around. It was also very dark. As a child and even then, at eighteen, I was still terrified of the dark. I returned to our room and waited. He came back almost two hours after I went in to get changed.

"Where were you?" I was hysterical. "I was so scared that something had happened to you!"

That is when he first reared his head.

"Stop being a bitch!"

No one had ever called me that before. It was stunning to hear it from my husband on my wedding night.

"I went for a swim in the pool."

"Liar." I could sense his deception. "I was at the pool. You weren't there."

"Well, I actually went to the beach." Despite his denial, I knew he was lying. He had lost my trust. We did not consummate our marriage until months later.

The next morning, he was back to his charming self. I wanted ice cream for breakfast to help with my nausea, so we went to town to get some and walk around. I was so hurt, though I didn't show it. I was also a little scared. Something didn't feel right.

When we came back to Jacksonville, we told my parents right away about the pregnancy. I was already calling it "she" as I knew with every fiber of my being that I was carrying Sabrina. It did not surprise my parents when we informed them, as they had already suspected it. We also told them we would look for an apartment as soon as possible. The next day, we stumbled upon a second-story apartment with two bedrooms and a total living space of 1100 square feet. I had quit Taco Bell and was currently working as a hostess at The Olive Garden. By far, it was the hardest and worst job I have ever had. Sometimes I used to stand there for hours without seeing even one customer. This was not well-suited for someone with ADHD.

Because Daniel and I had the same schedule, it meant that we only required one car between the two of us. Larry, Daniel's brother, started working and needed a car. We lent him our Geo Metro. It was supposed to be a temporary arrangement. Several months later, my parents were hanging out for the weekend in Saint Augustine. They invited us to join them, but we needed money for gas to get there. I pointed out to Daniel that we are still paying for insurance as well as making payments on the car that his brother had been using for months.

"Perhaps he should at least pay half of the insurance if he's going to keep driving it? We can take that sixty bucks and go to Saint Augustine."

Daniel agreed, and off to his parent's home we went. Daniel and I went to talk to Larry when we arrived. The words that we spoke barely left our mouths when we witnessed this grown man yelling for his mommy.

"Mom, Mama!!!"

Juana came running. "Que paso?"

"They are asking me for money!"

The moment we realized what was happening, we hurriedly attempted to clarify the situation to her. Her reaction was unexpected as her head spun a full 360 degrees. I thought my eyes had deceived me. She sternly ordered us to stop talking. At the top of her lungs, she yelled that I was nothing but a whore. Her voice was not her own. In a shocking statement, she claimed that the baby I carried inside me was not her son's, but instead, belonged to a black man. I kept trying to calm her down, but she was off her rocker. I was in shock. My mother-in-law thought I had been unfaithful to my husband with a black man. She swore up and down that my baby would be a mulatto.

"You better go," Albert advised.

"If you throw me out of this house, I will not be back for a very long time," I said.

"You better go."

My first experience with a complete demonic manifestation left me bewildered and confused as to what exactly I was observing. The things that were coming out of her mouth were from beyond this realm. I wish so much now that I knew then what I was looking at. I would not return to that home for years.

I went to my sister Nicole's home for comfort. Daniel stayed with his parents. He never protected me or defended me, just let his mother go off on me over and over. I was so heartbroken. He eventually picked me up from my sister's place. He had nothing to say about why he didn't protect me. I was four months pregnant.

Around this same time, Daniel got a job as a waiter at a country and western bar. There, he met a private investigator and his pregnant wife. He chatted them up and told them his wife was also pregnant. Because of his charming nature, the husband offered to train him as a private eye.

One night, I had a dream. It had the same sensation as the dream I had with Dustin and his pregnant girlfriend. I dreamt of six numbers. When I woke up, I remembered them distinctly. Could these be lottery numbers? I had prayed so hard as a child to win the lottery that it felt like a real possibility. I played the numbers. In Florida, we only had lotto once a week in those days. They didn't come out. I thought, well, then it was just a silly dream.

It was during the following week when I was enjoying a slice of chicken pizza at Çiçi's Pizza that I noticed the lottery numbers for that week being displayed on the screen. They were the exact same numbers as my dream. Playing the numbers for two consecutive weeks never occurred to me. When we got home, I threw up the pizza. I didn't tell anyone the story for years because who was going to believe it?

I was house-sitting for my parents when a detective from the Orange Park Police Department called to ask if Daniel was available. I immediately had a bad feeling.

"Yes, he is, Detective. One moment please. Daniel! There is a detective on the phone for you."

"I have to take this. I promise to tell you everything when I hang up," was Daniel's answer as he went into a room and closed the door behind him. My heart was about to pound out of my chest. Daniel came out of the room and straight to me.

"We need to talk. I have a problem. I have been going through the TCBY drive-thru without my pants on." He had to explain it to me three times because I swore I wasn't hearing correctly. Something happened that he didn't want to discuss, but he had this issue since he was a child. I asked him if there were other incidents. He said yes, that he had done the same thing in a few other drive-thrus; and sometimes he would ask women for directions without his pants on.

My guidance told him that honesty was the best policy and that he should confess. To be as open as possible to keep himself safe. To my astonishment, he followed my directions to a tee. The next day, we went down to the police station. The whole thing was resolved within months. He received probation, and he miraculously wasn't put on the sex offender registry. However, his arrest presented serious issues with private investigation. Prior to entering his plea, he could obtain a temporary private investigator's license. He was able to use it while undergoing training and working in Florida. Once his case was registered with the state, he would lose his license.

My pregnancy was extremely difficult. I puked for eight months. I threw up so much the first three months that I lost ten pounds. Not to worry, I would soon gain them back. That I had someone else's life inside of me was a fact not lost on me. I took pregnancies seriously and did not smoke or drink except for a couple of sips at Christmas. There was always a lot of pressure from my mother to drink alcohol, and it made her so happy when I did. I also didn't touch things like bleach and other cleaning chemicals.

Daniel did a case in Miami. When he returned, I could feel that he had been intimate with another woman and said nothing. He was obviously very sorry because he was doting on me hand and foot. I could also feel that he didn't enjoy it. I was hoping it wouldn't happen again. Until death do us part, right?

We were living paycheck to paycheck after I stopped working. The values that I hold are unique to me, and I understand they may not resonate with everyone. My whole life, all I wanted to be was a stay-at-home mom, but that opportunity only happened a few times. Because of my sensitivity, I tire easily, and I don't have the energy that others do. I knew I could never be one of those women who worked full time and took care of their house and children, but I didn't have a choice. I spent most of my child-rearing days working full time. I worked odd hours and days, so my children basically raised themselves. I truly believe with every fiber of my being that if a woman wants to stay home with her babies, she should have the opportunity to do so. Nurturing our children should be a priority. That doesn't mean we create a law that says all moms must stay home, but perhaps create the opportunity for those who want to make child-rearing a priority. Although some may argue that this would result in more welfare moms, it is crucial to raise a generation of strong and well-rounded individuals, which is not currently happening.

Daniel worked a lot as a private investigator and as a part-time DJ. Sabrina was due on Valentine's Day. On February twenty-second, they planned to induce me. The doctors started the Pitocin drip around 9 a.m., but by 5 p.m. nothing had happened. They stopped trying. I was told that I would stay the night in a hospital room in case I went into labor. At around 1 a.m. on February twenty-third, I got up to use the restroom. As I was exiting the bathroom, a nurse peeked her head in.

"Oh, you are up, good. I want to check you for signs of labor."

"I'm fine. I just went to the bathroom," was my reply. As I'm writing this, it is 11:23. Twenty-three becomes a huge number for me later in life.

"Well, I have to check you anyway."

I laid down for the examination and, to my surprise, I was three centimeters dilated.

"We are going to move you to a birthing suite."

Really? This was labor? My periods were far worse than this. My periods were so incredibly painful that I would be out of commission for one day a month. So painful that tears would stream down my face uncontrollably. My dad used to get so upset seeing his baby suffer like that. Feeling his concern was worse than the pain itself.

I got moved to the birthing suite. The medical staff scheduled me for an epidural, so I received one. While the contractions were not as terrible as my periods, I went through with the epidural as recommended. My obstetrician was Filipino and very Catholic. She surprised us with a prayer just before delivery, making me grateful because we couldn't pray at home and my mom was there. Both my mom and Daniel were there. Shortly after this prayer, divine energy entered the room. I thought I was high on the epidural. I would find out in the future that this was not a side effect of the epidural. What I perceive to be Yahweh, God, had entered the room.

As a result of tearing, I bled profusely to where a blood transfusion should have been necessary. Unfortunately, I did not receive one. I could feel every stitch when I was being sewn up. Nowadays, I wonder if that is why God was there that day. I'm not exaggerating about the amount of blood there was at that birth. It was hair-raising. Despite all this, it was the best day of my life. Not only was Yahweh, God, there, but the amazing emotions one feels when they meet their child for the first time made it so incredibly special. It was magical. She weighed eight pounds and twelve ounces.

Daniel was great. Because of the numbness in my legs, I couldn't move. He came to my rescue by picking me up from the bed and placing me on the toilet several times with great care. I was so grateful that he was strong and built like a truck. Daniel's job planned on transferring him to Miami for cases as he spoke Spanish. Unfortunately, his criminal case caught up to him and, as a result, he lost his temporary private investigator license.

Because we were moving to Miami, my parents and I went to South Florida and toured every new single home construction site. They eventually settled on a home in a neighborhood called Harmony Lakes in the town of Davie, Florida, which was located north of Miami and West of Ft. Lauderdale. The day before we were supposed to move, we got the news. Because of his licensing issues, he was no longer being transferred to Miami. The firm he worked for was rapidly expanding. He was allowed to take cases in Mississippi where no permits were necessary. He would also take up cases in Louisiana because of the lenient laws over there. We could choose either state to live in. I was quite familiar with Louisiana, as my father was a jazz fanatic. I had spent many vacations in New Orleans. Daniel and I had even been there with my parents during my pregnancy with Sabrina.

I knew nothing about Mississippi, so we went to live in Louisiana. The energy in New Orleans was terrible, which is why I didn't want to live there. I looked at a map; and Lafayette sounded lovely. Sabrina was six weeks old. We rented a very quaint townhome. I settled into being the perfect housewife. On some days, I was so bored that I regularly refolded all the clothes in all the drawers neatly. We were barely making it financially. We ate a lot of Hamburger Helper after I learned how to make it.

From time to time, we would get sent on cases out of state. I would go with him on those investigations and help him with surveillance and driving while he filmed. I even did some of his reports for him. Sometimes I did some investigating myself. I was eighteen. No one ever suspected I was a private investigator's assistant. I frequently had to check on the expected location of the person we were investigating before starting a case.

"Yeah, my dad and him were friends in high school, and he would really like to reconnect with him, with her," was my most common excuse. Or, over the phone, "Hi this is FP&L calling. We have received reports of a power outage in your area. Would you mind going outside and telling me if you see anything unusual on the power line outside your home?" This was also useful to get billable hours. Many times, the person would never leave their home. If we didn't get video, the company he worked for would not get paid.

One night, I was on the phone with my mom. It was one of those conversations that went on and on. When I finally hung up, a feeling of severe dread entered my body. It occurred to me I hadn't seen Daniel for a while. I went upstairs. He was nowhere to be found. I checked all the rooms except for the baby's room because why would he be in there? She was sleeping. After a second and third search of the home, I finally went into Sabrina's room. I was not prepared for what I was about to see.

CHAPTER 7

Twenty-three

It was beyond belief. I was so shocked that I thought my eyes were deceiving me. But no, there was my husband sitting naked in Sabrina's bedroom window for the entire neighborhood to see. What was most shocking to me was that he had already been arrested for this. Didn't he learn his lesson? He was putting his family at risk. Didn't he care about us?

He immediately started apologizing. I was out of my mind. At that moment, I longed for my mother like never before. I couldn't comprehend how someone who was caught for a crime and escaped punishment could repeat the same thing. It was beyond my frame of reference.

It was a few days later that Daniel came to me. He said he wanted to quit his job and move back to Florida. I immediately agreed. I called my mom.

"Mom, can we come live with you for a little while?"

"Of course, honey; we love you," was my mom's reply.

In the Harmony Lakes subdivision, my parents purchased a large two-story, four-bedroom house. Harmony Lakes was a very appealing neighborhood. Despite the presence of some older townhomes within the community, the newer section was contemporary and trendy, featuring newer townhomes and spacious single-family homes. The list of amenities for the neighborhood was amazing. It included a large community pool, racquetball courts, a basketball court, a walking path, a playground, a community gazebo, and several serene lakes.

We looked at many homes. The formal dining set my mom owned was not only expensive but also large, so it was necessary to find a house with enough space for it. After searching for a home with a large dining room, they discovered that the home in Harmony Lakes was the only one that met their requirements. Formal meals held a special place in my mother's heart.

We skipped out on our lease and moved to Florida. Living with my mom was difficult. Sabrina was four months old when we moved in. I was still sleeping eighteen hours a day because I had lost so much blood giving birth. This went on for another two months.

Daniel found a job as a DJ, as well as entertaining kids. He dressed up in various character costumes. He was excellent at these jobs. In Spain, he had run his own bar at fifteen. Juana and her Spanish boyfriend owned two bars in the Canary Islands. One of the bars was run by Daniel.

I was sleeping one afternoon when I had an empathic dream. This dream had the same quality as the dream with the girl with long black hair and the one with the lottery numbers, so I knew it was serious. During my sleep, I dreamt that Daniel was swimming naked at the community pool across the street where there were children around. I bolted out of bed. I ran downstairs.

"Have you seen Daniel?" I asked my dad.

"He went to the pool."

My heart was in my throat. I couldn't run fast enough. Despite it being only a three-minute sprint to the community pool, in the state I was in, it felt like an hour had passed. When I got there, he was in the pool swimming in a pair of light gold silk briefs that left absolutely nothing to the imagination as they were completely see through. There were indeed many children around. I kept calling his name; he kept ignoring me. I told him if he didn't get out of the pool that I would call the police. That made him get out. I couldn't believe this was my husband. I made it clear to him that if he didn't return home in the next two minutes, I would have no choice but to involve the cops.

When I got back to my parent's house, I was hysterical. Based on his experience as a sexual crimes' detective, my father told me it was not uncommon for individuals who exhibit such behavior to continue doing it. My dad said he would eventually outgrow it and told me not to divorce him, to be patient. Taking my vows seriously was something that I always believed in. I had every intention of staying with my husband through sickness and in health, which is why I remained by his side. Daniel kept trying to convince me he was merely swimming in his underwear. I knew then that this would be an ongoing problem.

Shortly after this, I decided I needed a job. Depending financially on a man who exposes himself is a scary proposition. I went to a temporary staffing agency. My desired rate was seven dollars an hour. I had a job the next day at a jewelry manufacturer called Aurafin. Owned by a local family, they made jewelry which was sold at wholesale prices to places like Walmart, Mayors, QVC, and other large retailers. They sold many of their pieces under warranty. I worked in the returns department. I inspected the jewelry that customers returned to determine if it was repairable. If the piece was irreparable, we would provide the customer with a new one.

One weekend, we went to visit Daniel's parents in Orange Park, Florida. We were going to hang out with my good friend Tammy. Tammy had recently become obsessed with male review shows. When my mother-in-law heard this, she said, "I want to go." So, I, of course, agreed to go as well.

The day of the male review show, Daniel started acting very strange. He sat me down and said, "If you can go to a show with male strippers, when we go back to South Florida, I can become a stripper." I thought he was kidding. No, he was serious. I told him I didn't want him to become a stripper. He said that if I went to this show, he would become one. There was no way I was not going. Tammy and Juana were so excited, I couldn't let them down. The review show was fun and nothing inappropriate happened. When we got back, Daniel once again told me he would become a male stripper. I thought, well, maybe he won't have to expose himself anymore. Daniel kept his promise and began working at the male review venue nearby, despite my objections. This truly hurt our marriage a lot.

I am not the jealous type. The pain never stemmed out of that. It was because by not adhering to my wishes he had broken my trust. This hurt stayed with me for at least six months. What shocked me the most was how little he earned from stripping. He made more money being a DJ and dressing up in costumes for children's parties. Then, without my knowledge, he began dancing for men and doing private strip-a-grams. He made as much money in one strip-a-gram as he did dancing for ladies for four hours. The big money started coming in when he began dancing for men.

I convinced my parents to help us buy a house. I couldn't live with my mother any longer. One night while she was drunk, she slapped her adult daughter across the face for absolutely no reason. I had to get out of there. We found a starter home just a few neighborhoods away from my parents. It was still within walking distance. It was a two-bedroom, single story villa in a neighborhood called Scarborough. The neighborhood was beautiful. Everyone had a white picket fence, with nice sidewalks to go for walks. There was a community pool and many more amenities.

Daniel, a go-getter, landed me a job as a private investigator after I worked at Aurafin for a year. I went from making seven dollars per hour to making twelve. Despite working long hours, I didn't receive overtime pay because I was classified as an independent contractor. Even on my day off, I had to turn in all my reports and videos to the office after working six days a week. Every case had to be pre-cased. I usually did this one or two evenings before the case started. My workload consisted solely of workman's compensation and liability cases. I was hired for one bounty hunt. I found the fugitive because one of his friends thought I was looking to hook up. The friend had no clue that the twenty-year-old he was dealing with worked for a firm capable of sending a hunter after his friend. He was caught; the firm kept the bounty.

People who filed workman's comp cases were caught engaging in activities that they claimed they couldn't do because of their injuries, such as playing ball, working off the books, gardening, and lifting heavy objects. The cases started at 6 a.m. unless we had intel that told us otherwise. Many were far away. I investigated the tri-county area, Palm Beach, Broward, and Miami-Dade counties. I was fortunate enough to live in Broward, which was in the middle of the three counties. My home was conveniently near major highways. My usual routine involved waking up between four and four-thirty in the morning. I remember thinking, "I can't believe I'm waking up at these hours again." After high school, I had promised myself to never wake up so early again. Twelve bucks an hour was a lot better than seven. So, early I would rise, get dressed, and go straight to the gas station. The number one rule of private investigation is that no matter how much gas you have left, you top off before every case.

I learned early on not to take my eyes off the house, because the moment you did, you missed your target. I still would get paid, but too many cases without video could get you fired. I would drive to the location in my Ford Taurus with limo-tinted windows and just sit there. I would put a sunscreen on the front windshield. Turn off the car. Sometimes I waited for hours for the person I was investigating to move. It was hard sitting in the Florida heat. Many times, I felt like I was going to pass out. I lost a lot of weight. I think I went down to a size three. One day, while out on a case, I got a phone call from Daniel.

"I just won $1,500 at the casino."

"What casino are you talking about?"

"I went to the casino after work today and won $1,500. You know, the Seminole casino on 441." Wow, that was very cool. The next week, he won $1,200. And so, his gambling addiction started. A few weeks later, I started noticing money disappearing out of our joint account. Then he maxed out our credit cards. I was getting concerned.

It was February 23rd, Sabrina's second birthday. We threw a big party at our small home. Daniel dressed up as Barney or Dora the Explorer. My in-laws came down from Orange Park, Florida. It was a beautiful event. The casino where Daniel played had the first high stakes bingo hall in the country, which my bingo-crazy mother-in-law loved. The Seminole Indian tribe opened its first bingo hall in 1979 on their reservation. Juana begged and pleaded that we all go to play bingo. My mom was even going. Daniel didn't want to play bingo. I gave him forty dollars to play slots because he had trouble managing his gambling. I had taken his atm card and credit cards away.

After we settled everyone in the bingo hall, I went to check on him. When I approached his slot machine, he had three hundred and forty dollars! We were living paycheck to paycheck because of his previous gambling practices. That was a lot of money for people who are living paycheck to paycheck.

"Dan, please cash that out. That is a lot of money," I said.

"I know what I'm doing. Leave me alone," he snarled at me. I never want to upset anyone, so I just went back to the bingo hall. Bingo had only been going for about ten minutes when Daniel barged in, shouting at the top of his lungs that he had won twenty-three thousand dollars. Coincidentally, it was February 23rd; he was 23 years old, and it was our daughter's birthday, so the number 23 immediately became my lucky number. It wasn't until decades later that I would discover Psalm 23. The Lord has always been my shepherd.

The players in the Bingo hall were shushing him. Most gamblers only care about their own gambling when they are gambling. This was no exception. My mom and mother-in-law kept playing Bingo. I got up and divided my bingo cards between them. I had to go see for myself if this was true.

It was. We had to wait for the money for quite some time. Daniel requested ten thousand dollars in cash, which was the maximum amount allowed. The remaining amount was issued by check. My eyes were drawn to the poker tables while we waited. My mother-in-law mentioned that she was a regular at the Tampa casino, where she played poker often. She offered to teach me. We were able to sit next to each other without having trouble. That night, I learned how to play poker. I was smitten.

My parents loaned us the down-payment for the house, which resulted in us being in debt for approximately twenty thousand dollars. We gave both our mothers $500, and when we got home, Juana hustled us out of another $500 for Albert, which, of course, we gave gladly. She then tried to get another $500 for Daniel's brother. I had to put on the brakes. Juana absolutely didn't care that we needed that money to get out of debt. I had never met people like this before. Years earlier, Juana had fallen behind on their mortgage because of her Bingo habit. I immediately offered to sell my Honda Civic, which was paid off. I wasted no time in giving her the money for three mortgage payments. After paying off our debt to my parents, Daniel got himself a computer and speaker for his DJ gear.

We started playing poker regularly. I had declared Wednesday night to be my poker night. Daniel stayed home with Sabrina. It was so inexpensive to play poker because the stakes were, I kid you not, twenty-five and fifty cents. You could easily play for hours on twenty dollars and even if you had a terrible night, you would only lose forty or sixty bucks.

When I was twelve, I started smoking. I felt like I didn't belong at my new private school; my aim was to be cool. I smoked occasionally since then but quit while carrying Sabrina. At the Seminole Poker Room, you had the option to choose between a smoking or non-smoking table. The non-smoking tables were boring. The folks were half asleep. If you wanted to party, you had to be at the smoking tables. It was full of folks joking with each other and genuinely having a good time. That is how I started smoking on Wednesday nights.

I continued with my private investigation work for a while, putting in long days of twelve to fourteen hours. I was beyond exhausted. The company also kept sending me out on cases where previous investigators had gotten burned without telling me. It is important for the company to disclose any failed attempts by previous investigators, as the person being investigated may be wary and require a different approach. On one such occasion, the person sent out his brother, who looked a lot like him. He tried to run me off the road. In another case, they didn't inform the investigator, and he was beaten up, leaving him in the hospital. When I complained about this practice, it fell on deaf ears. I became concerned about my safety. I carried a stun gun as I was not allowed to deal with firearms, per my intuition, until I was much older and wiser. Currently, I own two guns. A nine-millimeter and a hunting rifle. I take owning a gun as a great responsibility. I make sure I practice a few times a year.

One of our cars broke down in May that year. Daniel's gambling had maxed out our credit cards again. We had forty dollars left and decided to each play twenty dollars in poker to see if a miracle would happen. Daniel was a horrible poker player. He busted out right away. It took me a little longer. When I went to check on him, people had surrounded him.

"What happened?" I asked.

"I somehow managed to withdraw twenty dollars from the ATM. I put it in, hit max bet, and I hit the jackpot!" was his response.

"How much was it?"

"Twenty-nine thousand." My life, so weird.

We fixed the car. That summer, we vacationed in Spain. We started a DJ business, which we advertised in the Yellow Pages. The cost of a small ad took me by surprise, as it was thousands of dollars. Google wasn't a thing. Before Google, the Yellow Pages was used to find phone numbers and addresses. We put a good amount of money in our savings account as well.

CHAPTER 8

Feces on My Face

I was shooting the breeze with some poker dealers. That is how I found out how much money they made. Their pay was comparable to mine, but those dealers also dealt tournaments. I became totally fascinated with poker, and I believed working as a dealer would improve my skills. When I heard of a poker dealer school, I left private investigating and started training to become a dealer. It was fifteen hundred dollars for a six-week course.

Poker became my life. My effective poker playing skills led to a great deal of success. I was regarded as a skilled local player. My intuitive abilities were unknowingly contributing to my success. I thought everyone had them. After I became a poker dealer, Daniel's gambling got so out of control that I had to pay all our bills on the four hundred and seventy-five dollars a week I was making. To even get a couple of hundred out of Daniel meant World War III. It got so bad that one of our vehicles got repossessed. Our savings were wiped out. He stopped showing up for gigs we booked for our business. Back when I was shy, there were times I had to do DJ work. It was a challenge and a very unpleasant experience for me.

After this, I gave Daniel an ultimatum. It worked. I naively believed it was over when he stopped gambling for a few weeks. We were physically intimate once during this time. Imagine my surprise when I didn't

63

get my period. I was so confused. We were only intimate one time... but sure enough; I was pregnant. Daniel resumed his gambling habit, worse than before, as soon as he found out. His multiple-day disappearances made me depressed. If it hadn't been for the depression, I would have easily had the best pregnancy of my life. I had so much energy that I actually started working out and did so for the first five months of the pregnancy. My son to this day is a gym rat.

My husband was angry that I was pregnant. He retaliated by ignoring me during the whole pregnancy. I was so depressed. He was so mean to me that a few days before my due date I took Sabrina and left to stay at my mom's. That night when we went to bed, I was tickling Sabrina. She was laughing so loudly and was so excited that she accidentally kicked my belly. A horrified look came over her. She had kicked it so hard that my belly bump was to the side and not in front of me.

I calmed her down, told her everything was going to be ok, and tucked her in.

As soon as I did that, I passed out.

When I woke up a few hours later at around 1 a.m., my belly was still a little askew. I went to the bathroom and there was blood.

I ran to my mom's room. "Mom, I'm bleeding!"

"Well, then you are in labor. I'll be right down," was her response.

I put Sabrina in bed with my dad while my mom was getting dressed. I didn't want her to wake up scared and not find me around. My mom then went downstairs and started squeezing oranges for orange juice, making coffee, and popped some bread in the toaster...

"Mom! I'm in labor, we have to go!"

"But I have to have my breakfast."

"Are you kidding? We have to go!" I knew my situation was dire, but I felt all would turn out fine. I could feel it.

"And I'm driving!" I told her. It was important to make sure I got to that hospital as soon as possible. Her putzing around wasn't reassuring me she would get me there on time. I was feeling very light cramps, which I recognized to be labor, once again thinking that my periods were much worse. When we arrived at the hospital, the nurse checked my dilation. She informed me I was three centimeters. She also mentioned that they would transfer me to a birthing suite and if there was no progress by 7am, they would administer Pitocin. I kept calling Daniel. There was no answer. I knew I could never forgive him if he missed the birth of his son. The medical staff hooked me up to all kinds of machines. Meanwhile, the anesthesiologist was summoned for the epidural.

"I have to go get more medicine, but you are only three centimeters, so it will be fine. I will be right back," he told me. The anesthesiologist wasn't gone for maybe ten minutes when all hell broke loose. Machines started going crazy. A nurse came in.

"We lost the baby's heartbeat."

What happened next was the biggest miracle of all miracles. My mother started praying! Yes, my mom the atheist, on her knees, praying in a corner. Maybe she was just a pretend atheist to appease my dad? She would become more spiritual after that.

About twelve nurses came flying in. Everyone was working in unison, trying to figure out what happened. As usual in emergency situations, I remained calm. Maybe I stayed calm because I knew how it was going to turn out. I didn't have any bad feelings during the entire saga. Not when Sabrina kicked me, not when I saw blood, not when I was driving, and not even when the machines were going nuts. In that sense, being intuitive is beneficial. However, there are days I wake up knowing something bad will occur. On those days, I have to gather all of my bravery to get out of bed. It just happened two days ago. I once again wished I had stayed in bed all day and waited for a better day.

A few minutes later, a nurse said, "We have him back. This baby is in a hurry to get out. He moved down the birthing canal so quickly we lost him for a moment. We are calling the doctor. You are ready to give birth." I had been in that birthing suite for less than thirty minutes.

"Oh, and we apologize, but you can no longer get an epidural. You are too far along."

"Wait, what?!" The idea of a natural birth never crossed my mind, leaving me mentally unprepared for what was about to happen. The labor itself didn't hurt. It wasn't comfortable by any means. What took the longest was for the doctor to get there. It took like an hour and a half. I knew I was ready to push. To this day, I still don't understand how, in the name of profit, a mother getting ready to push a baby out has to wait. If profit was not involved, any obstetrician could have delivered the baby.

They say that giving birth is a pain you don't remember. Now I know why. Because you don't want to remember it! Contractions I could handle. The crowning of the baby's head, that was something else. The only physical pain I have felt that was worse than that is passing a kidney stone. I would rather give natural birth to five babies than pass a kidney stone.

I am extremely blessed to have wide hips. Birth, for me, involved only one or two pushes. I thought I was being torn apart. After Noah came out, I couldn't bring myself to look at him. I was so physically hurt. As I took a quick glance, I couldn't help but notice that he was born with an erection, which made me wonder if that was a normal occurrence. I couldn't help but chuckle. The situation became less serious after that. My mom was so happy.

"He's so handsome. Look at his dimples, blond hair, and those blue eyes!"

My son was born good looking. He still turns heads wherever he goes. He even had a six-pack and very defined leg muscles. I had never seen a muscular baby before. It also shocked me how well I felt. I could move my legs. I bled a small fraction of what I did the first time. Noah and I had an invisible umbilical cord. When they were bringing him back from his circumcision, I could feel him coming down the hallway. I will never forget how he was trembling and sobbing. He has since thanked me a dozen times for his circumcision, but man did I have my doubts at that moment.

Disappointment filled my heart when I realized Daniel had missed his son's birth. After he was born, my intuition told me to call the neighbors to see if he was home yet. It was after 5 a.m. My neighbor was actually an OB-GYN nurse at that same hospital. She called back to let me know she had found Dan at the house and that he was on his way.

By the afternoon, Daniel said, "I have to go, but I will be back tomorrow to pick you up."

The nurses informed me at around 7 p.m. that I was being discharged. Wait. I just gave birth fourteen hours ago. Daniel didn't answer my call, which was not surprising. It was so humiliating that I had to call my parents to come get me from the hospital. They brought Sabrina with them and then they dropped all three of us off at home. So, there I was on my first night after giving birth with a newborn, a toddler, and zero help. I felt so alone. Daniel did not come home until the morning. He was shocked to find us at home. He had been out gambling all night. I knew at that moment that I had to divorce this person. He was all excited because he had won five thousand dollars. He showed me the money and the paperwork. Money to me does not imply happiness. I couldn't care less how much money he won. Noah, however, needed some things. Not having had a baby shower, I had very little for him. I told Dan we were going shopping. I got him clothes and a stroller.

I was going to breastfeed Noah, but after a few days, my nipples were bleeding terribly. By the time I realized I could not breastfeed Noah, Daniel had gambled away what was left of the five thousand dollars he had won. I remember calling my boss a week after giving birth. "Will, please put me on the schedule for Monday. I don't have any money to feed my baby." Will, my boss, was shocked. "Of course, whatever you need." When Noah was just nine days old, I returned to work.

Daniel continued to gamble without restraint. I knew I had to make a plan to get divorced. The only way I could afford all the bills was to get a second job. My parents had already been helping financially, as Daniel contributed nothing to the pot. While I was working as a poker dealer, I couldn't work for competitors, but I was allowed to deal on casino ships because they gambled in international waters. We had two ships in town: the Sea Escape and the SunCruz. One night, I spoke to the SunCruz manager, who gave me an audition. He said, "I don't need another dealer, but my high limit players prefer a pretty face, so I'm hiring you for your looks."

How well would that go over in this day and age? I made as much in three or four hours there as I did at my other job. They also promoted me to tournament dealer at my land-based job. Most dealers had to wait years to make it into tournaments. They chose only the best dealers for this, of course, unless you went into the office and closed the door. I don't know exactly what those girls did behind that closed door, but shortly afterwards they would get promoted to tournament dealer. That was not my scene. Between both jobs and my promotion, I could afford all my bills on my own.

Somewhere around this time, I started experiencing a strange phenomenon. I was able to predict cards that were coming off the deck. Whenever this one particular young man would come in, I could call every card off the deck. I said to him, "You want to see something cool?" I successfully guessed every card in the deck. It happened twice with him. After that, it was years before I saw him again. When I finally saw him again, he was watching me deal. His appearance had changed drastically, and he had all kinds of face and neck tattoos. When I got up, I went to greet him.

"How did you do that when you were calling every card off the deck?" he asked.

"I have no clue. It just happened," I answered.

"You were cheating, weren't you?"

"What? I was absolutely not cheating. I swear on my children."

"I don't believe you." He walked away from me. Once again, I hurt someone with my abilities. Ugh.

My relationship with Daniel had been strained for a while. One night, things finally reached their breaking point. On that particular day, a colleague from Panama had gifted me two of his tuxedo shirts, which were part of our uniform back then, as they did not fit him. As it is customary in the Latino community, I thanked him with a kiss on the cheek.

That night, I gave Daniel a dose of his own medicine. I went out without telling him. A friend of mine and I went to play cards until past 1 a.m. I didn't tell Daniel where I was going as he never told me. When I got home, Daniel was out of his mind. He called me a slut. He accused me of kissing some guy at work. Then he grabbed me by the throat and put me up against the wall. In a disgusting act, he took the dog feces he had in his hand and wiped it all over my face. As he held me against my will, forcefully pulling out the phone from the wall and locking all the doors, I found myself trapped and unable to escape.

The worst part is that Sabrina saw the whole thing. She was only four. Diffusing the situation became a priority. I remained calm, as I always do. I started reading Daniel. As I could never feel his emotions, I always had to be careful around him. I watched his every move. I tried to find an avenue to get him to calm down. For over an hour, he continued to yell at me until he finally calmed down. He wouldn't let me leave. Three long hours passed before I was finally able to convince him I needed water. I told him I loved him, that I would never leave him, that I forgave him, whatever I needed to say to find a way out.

I wouldn't find out until years later that Daniel had a boyfriend who was obsessed with him. A wealthy butler whom he met while dancing at the Copa, the local gay nightclub. This boyfriend had taken it upon himself to hire a private investigator to dig up dirt on me so he could have Daniel all to himself. This investigator had seen me give my co-worker a kiss on the cheek, but apparently had omitted the cheek part. That was not the only time I was followed. Another night I went out dancing with some girls. I was also followed.

After many pleadings, Daniel finally relented and went to get me a glass of water. I didn't hesitate. I bolted to the front door. Somehow, I unlocked the two locks at the same time. By the time he got to me, I was running across the street to a neighbor's house. The cops were upset when they saw my face covered in dog feces. They were taking him in, and they were not being nice about it. Daniel and I never lived together as husband and wife again after charges were filed. I absolutely could not let my daughter think this was ok. I also knew that if she hadn't been a witness, I would probably have swept it under the rug because my wedding vows were everything to me.

The last year with Daniel had been absolute torture. He would scream at me every single day until I cried. He would constantly threaten me with taking my kids from me. I would get on my knees daily and pray for a way out. Sometimes I stayed on my knees praying for hours. I have no doubts now that staying in a bad situation is not what God wants for you, regardless of how many vows and promises you have made. My opinion now is that marriage is a human concept, and it is not for everyone. My beliefs include that those who embark on the journey of marriage should be spiritually and physically healthy, otherwise, it is just a matter of time.

I love the concept of marriage, but I have seen so many unions that are not right and these stubborn people stay together because of religion, finances, and so many other externalities, sacrificing their long-term happiness. All of us have beliefs that simply aren't true. Many humans die with these faulty frameworks, and some get stuck in another dimension because of it. I believe that it produces spirits, ghosts. Folks like mediums counsel these spirits to help them get to Heaven, the astral plane, the field. Once again, I must reiterate that these are solely my beliefs. It is quite probable and highly likely that they are incorrect, but it is what helps me sleep at night. If your Bible, Qur'an, Torah, helps you sleep at night, I will not judge you for it. I will be happy for you.

I experienced severe panic attacks after my attack from Daniel. Whenever a guest would yell at me, I would start having a panic attack. I would have to be removed from the table. I would eventually drop the charges because I was so afraid that Daniel would kill me and my kids if I didn't. This was a fear I would live with for a very long time.

CHAPTER 9

Mike

My regular daily schedule involved working at the Seminole Indian Casino each morning from 10 a.m. to 4 p.m. Before my shift on the SunCruz casino cruise ship, I would take a dinner break at an IHOP near the boat. My shift on the SunCruz lasted until 1 or 2 a.m., depending on if it was a weekday or weekend. I had one day off a week.

The day Daniel went to jail, I caught the eye of a young man at the IHOP. He was good-looking and extremely confident. It turns out that IHOP was a dining hall for a halfway house. His name was Michael H. He had been sentenced for bank robbery and had spent almost three years in prison before being released. He got three years because he didn't use a weapon. Michael and I started having dinner together every night. When I shared with Michael H. the details of what was happening with my first husband, he became outraged and vowed to protect me from any harm or danger.

Following the last incident, I wasted no time in consulting a divorce lawyer and starting the divorce process. Noah was just six weeks old when this all happened. Postpartum depression set in. Postpartum depression has a very unexpected side effect. You absolutely cannot and will not touch your baby. You will come up with every excuse under the sun. Bless Michael H. for being great with kids. He truly is like a chil-

71

dren's shepherd. Currently, he takes care of another man's child while raising his own daughter. He is so amazing. He truly enjoys children. People like that should have children.

Michael H. was fearless. We talked for about six weeks before anything happened between us. I can't just be with someone. I'm an empath. We operate on many levels, and intimacy starts with trust for me. The halfway house was only a temporary arrangement; it is housing while you look for a job and a permanent living situation. Michael was feeling the weight of finding a job, so I offered him a place to live with me. Many empaths live on feeling. I felt safe with Michael H., and he treated me like an absolute princess.

I had just moved into a new four-bedroom home. My mom was truly an exceptional force of nature. She helped me sell my last home by-owner in one day for a very nice profit. Not only that, but she even held an open house. She had so much energy; she was never tired. One of her admirable qualities was that she refused to ask others to do anything that she herself wouldn't do. However, one of her prominent tendencies was to ask others for favors. If she met anyone, she was trying to find something they could do for her. In eight out of ten times, that person was bending over backwards to do things for my mother. It was so bizarre to witness. My sister Hazel was the same way. If I ask you for a favor, it's because I really need your help.

Michael, much like my mom, was always meeting new people and making moves. That was when I started paying attention. When we would go out to bars, if a guy would look at me, he would absolutely lose his mind. Almost getting violent. That scared me. I was exhausted. I was working one hundred and ten hours a week to keep everything afloat, as Michael had trouble keeping jobs because of his temper. To boot, I found out I was pregnant. Holy Moly.

My pregnancy was difficult, I kept fainting due to low iron levels. My mother was kind enough to provide me with delicious meals of lentil soup and beef liver. That resolved it, but not before I had to stop working. Even on the cruise ship, I would get seasick. We were so desperate for money that I sold my regular clothes at a flea market. My parents were helping where they could. Savannah was born on August eighteenth 2001. I had a natural delivery because I felt so good after giving birth to Noah without the epidural.

She only took two pushes, but again the crowning of that baby, my GOD! Savannah was born jaundiced. She was so yellow. She looked like something from out of this world. They had to take her for treatment and kept her for observation. I was in the hospital for two and a half days with her. She responded to the treatment quickly.

I have never in my life before or after turned a television on at 9 a.m. On September 11, 2001, I awoke at 9 a.m. My body stood up and on its own turned on the television. It was on a local station. I stood there and observed a tower of The World Trade center with copious amounts of smoke coming out of it. As I stood there watching for maybe a minute or two, a second airplane crashed into the second tower. At that moment, I felt we were under attack.

I wasn't afraid. I knew everything would be ok, but I could feel the energy of the planet change. That was hard because I didn't understand what I was feeling. The same thing happened when COVID-19 first hit. The collective worries of the entire world have a tendency to decrease the overall vibration, which can be challenging for those who are sensitive.

Savannah was three weeks old. In my mind, I started getting organized. Michael was not working during that time. He stayed home with Noah and the baby while I went to get Sabrina. When I arrived at the school to pick up my child, I was only the second or third parent there. I noticed the long line of parents waiting to pick up their kids that had wrapped around the entire building when Sabrina was retrieved from her classroom. I was thanking God on my way out because standing in a long line to get my daughter would have sent my anxiety through the roof as I would not only experience my anxiety but the anxiety of others as well.

I took whatever money we had left to a Winn Dixie supermarket where I stocked up on diapers, formula, and, strangely, Nutter Butter cookies, which I had never previously had, but found to be very comforting during those times. I never got them again until COVID-19 in 2020.

It was a relief to feel the camaraderie that everyone had during 9/11, after experiencing their concern. Nearly everyone had American flags on their cars. Feeling the country coming together was so incredibly beautiful, one of the best experiences of my life. It is just a shame that it takes a tragedy of that magnitude to bring this out in people.

Michael H. kept getting into things that didn't feel good to me. I started taking some space. A bar that my coworkers frequented after work had a video game machine that was a quarter per play. The terminal had many types of games. I spent many hours there just to avoid him. After a few weeks of doing this, Mike L. started showing up at this place nightly. I knew Mike because he was my favorite Poker Tournament Director. He worked for our competitor's day cruise ship, The Seascape. He prided himself on transparency. Previous poker managers who were immoral had been fleecing players for a long time across the country. The idea of transparency was something that I found very appealing. The players were made aware of the exact allocation of the money. I love righteousness.

I couldn't believe my eyes. Mike had done a total body transformation. He had lost like a hundred pounds and looked amazing! Before I got pregnant with Savannah, I had suspected he was interested in me, but when I went to see him, he didn't feel the same way—as I can feel the emotions of others. What actually happened is that he met a bartender a day or two before and thought she was his one. We were talking nightly. My coworkers started saying that he had a crush on me. I told them, "Nah, we have been down this road before." As we walked out together one night, he surprised me by planting a gentle kiss on my neck. He gave me his phone number. I was in shock. I had no idea this was going this way. Then he went to get into his car, a special edition electric blue Acura TL. I was shaking my head. This guy had so much swag. On my way home, I rolled down my window, took one more look at his number, and threw it out. I have limited photographic memory. I had taken a picture of his number with my mind.

I was under so much pressure to make money. Mike dealt at a home game that had been going on for years. I thought I should ask him if I could deal there too, though that game gave me such a horrible vibe. Mike's phone number flashed in my mind: 9292908, before area codes. My curiosity got the best of me. I started wondering if I had actually taken a picture of his number. I realized I had indeed taken a picture of it when he answered. What a stupid idea, I thought. I most definitely didn't want to lead him on. Well, Mike took it upon himself to introduce me to alcohol. His ex-wife had been a bartender. Many nights, I became intoxicated. Months went by.

I can recall one night when I was definitely under the influence of alcohol, and in that condition I accepted his invitation to go back to his house. He lived in a two-story townhouse in Dania Beach, Florida, with a roommate. Dania was a town near the beach just south of Ft. Lauderdale. Mike loved roommates. Since nothing had happened the first time I visited his house, I felt safe. I know that my intoxication led to me sleeping with him. The lesson that I learned from this experience is to be less judgmental of others who make such claims. Before this, I had always been skeptical of those who did so. I decided after that I would never get drunk again, and it only happened a few more times after that. The truth about alcohol is complex and mankind is not ready to hear it yet.

I felt so comfortable with Mike, and we had what I now recognize as a past life connection. It was like I was with my family. It was a one-night stand, a slipup. I was going to end things with Michael H. anyway and had already started preparing him for my departure. I never contacted Mike after we slept together. I intended to end it there. Nine days later, I got a phone call from him.

"How come you never called me?" Because this was a one-night stand, or was it?

We ended the conversation with me agreeing to come over for a swim. By the time I slept with him for the second time, I was in love. Though I have experienced love on deeper levels since then, this was the first time I truly felt that I would take a bullet for someone. I was twenty-four years old. My spirit guides, or my delusion, as I used to call them, were not keen. I kept hearing that this was not a good match. We kept breaking up. I had broken things off with Michael H., but he still lived in my home. Most of the time, I spent the night at Mike L's. After supporting both Daniel and Michael H., I was beyond impressed that Mike could pay his own bills.

When I met Mike, he had his eye on this property near to where he lived. It was in horrible condition, worse than in a state of foreclosure. He figured that if he put fifty thousand dollars into it, he could easily make twenty or thirty thousand dollars profit. Did I want to take on this project with him? You wouldn't be able to tell by my humble surroundings, but remodeling and decorating are passions of mine, as I have an eye for natural beauty. I merely don't care about material possessions.

He bought the place. I went with him to the closing. Closings were not new to me. We were both well-versed in the laws and rules of real estate and bonded over it. I may lack formal education, but I make up for it by constantly learning. Although I hated school, I am passionate about learning. Once I was keen on buying my first home, I learned all there was to know and more about real estate.

Many things were happening around this time. When I turned twenty-five, Michael H. was back in jail for violation of probation. I was still working many jobs. I couldn't find a babysitter for Savannah. My mom had helped tremendously with Noah and Sabrina.

"I can't do it again. I'm getting too old," she told me.

I immediately replied, "Don't worry about it, Mom. I will figure it out."

During my sister Nicole's recent visit, she held Savannah. Telepathically, I heard, "Look how beautiful, mother and child." When I was pregnant with Savannah, I heard I was carrying my sister's child. I just sat there shaking my head. My sister Nicole had been the target of something sinister and couldn't have children. She is my protector. She saved my life many times as a child, and we have a bond that transcends this realm—as is clear every time we get together. It is a beautiful thing to watch. It has been quite a while since we could last see each other. Sadly, it has been three years now. She is full of energy like my mom. She heals with essential oils, and if karma is real I have seen her invoke it. So, watch out, don't piss her off.

Although Mike was accepting of my older children, he showed no interest in being involved with the baby. For him, Savannah was a deal breaker. I called up Nicole.

"Hi Nicole, Michael H. is back in jail and mom is getting too old for this stuff. Do you want to adopt Savannah?"

"I have to ask Tim. Can I call you right back?" It wasn't long. "We would love to adopt her."

"When can you be here?" I asked. I believe Natalie and her army husband, Tim, came down the next weekend. The pain from this ordeal was so extremely deep, I was unsure how to cope with it. I don't share pain because I don't want others to experience it.

My intuition again would try to tell me that this was a terrible matchup between Mike and I. I would cry out, "But I'm in love!" I truly thought that love could conquer all, that I could love enough for the both of us. Hollywood had programmed me to believe this. Mike had a tough childhood. He was born not being able to absorb formula and survived on liquified bananas. Because his mother had taken a certain medication while he was in the womb, he had a Jay Leno type chin and thus his nickname "The Chin."

His grandfather was deeply spiritual. I once touched his prayer books. To my surprise, we started to communicate telepathically. He was no longer alive. I, of course, thought I needed a psychiatrist. Mike's grandfather was awesome. He was truly a good man. He was here on a mission from God. He helped unionize the postal workers in New York. Certain sectors, such as postal workers, may benefit from having unions, but a capitalist company should not have them as they disrupt the free market model. All businesses based on the capitalist model should be allowed to run their course if we practice capitalism. I have worked for a company where the workers were unionized. At this company, the employees ran the show.

The employee would always threaten to report the supervisor to human resources (HR) and the union at the slightest disciplinary action taken against them. This could even be for an informal coaching. The supervisor would have to do this during their off time. Who in their right mind would start any sort of disciplinary action against these employees? HR just wanted a smooth sailing boat. There were employees there committing all kinds of violations, including theft. If we bail out businesses, we are no longer practicing capitalism in my humble opinion. Capitalism thrives on competition and on survival of the fittest. If some participants are getting preferential treatment, then the whole principle is compromised. I am apolitical, by the way. Politics are trying to divide people, so I stay out of them, but it was amazing to connect with this person every time I touched his books. Mike was a staunch Atheist.

Mike and I kept breaking up because he was desperate to have a child. I was done. I couldn't take care of my last one. Was he out of his mind? Oh, but it would be different, he would say, because he was the father. He was promising me the sun, moon, and stars.

CHAPTER 10

The Tunica Miracle

M ike took me on my first trip to Las Vegas. This vacation was to celebrate his niece's twenty-first birthday. I was going to be introduced to his family on this visit. His mother, sister, and niece came along. Mike mentioned to me several times that his mother was a very difficult person to deal with, always asking too many questions and laying on the Jewish guilt, which he claimed was typical of a Jewish mother. There was a funny coincidence. His sister and I had the same birthday, just in different years.

The memory of flying into Las Vegas and feeling the energy is unforgettable. This energy was definitely dark. But dark energy also feels delicious. It feels slightly dangerous and very exciting. My favorite part of working in casinos was feeling the energy. Casinos are some of the few places I can still feel energy. When I was young, I sensed the energy of everything. Every mountain, ocean, sea, river, and building felt distinct to me. It was awesome and something I miss deeply. I recently had a connection with an empath and when we connected, I could feel those things again, but it didn't last long as we didn't see each other.

I love Las Vegas. I love the energy. It revitalizes me and perks me right up. There I discovered Eggs Benedict, pecan pie, and, unfortunately on one evening, nickel slots. Penny slots weren't a thing yet. Mike took me to the New York New York casino where we played Monopoly

Nickel slots. Nickel slots could cost as little as five cents per line bet. A typical slot machine around that time had nine lines. We had an amazing time. It took us many hours of slot play to lose the hundred dollars we had set out to play. We felt like we won. Smart phones weren't a thing yet. This was world class entertainment.

In the industry, they call slot machines "the crack cocaine of gambling." That's how my fascination with video slots began. Luckily, it would be another year or two before they showed up in South Florida. I remember the first two. No one wanted to play them. I believe they were called Super Jackpot Party. Within months, they slowly started creeping in. While playing slots, I realized Savannah was no longer on my mind. It was a refreshing experience. Any relief from that pain was welcome. My parents and my intuition had been very stern with me as a child about cocaine, heroin, anything like that. They never said a word about cigarettes and gambling. It's how I coped.

After one of our longest breakups, Mike and I were invited to an impromptu trip to Tunica, Mississippi. Mike's bosses had discovered a casino with a single deck blackjack game where they paid regular odds. It was the only blackjack game like that in the country. They wanted him to drive. I was already on vacation. During the two weeks I was away from Mike, I had not eaten anything at all. When we reconciled, I took a week off. Many empaths fast when their world is off balance. It's how we cope.

We were departing the next day and driving with his boss, Adam, who intended to smoke weed the entire way. I never touched it. At that time, casinos tested for marijuana. I would never do anything to jeopardize my livelihood. The other two bosses were taking their own car.

The trip was fifteen hours. I got to witness Adam's true character during our one breakfast stop. He was a very mean-spirited man and employed this to get attention. When the waitress came over to top off his coffee and asked if he would like some more, he replied, "Little bitch, please." Mike and I were stunned. Mike looked at me and said "if she goes back there and the cook in the back was her boyfriend and she informed him of the situation, he wouldn't prevent him from beating Adam's ass. I was tuned into her. I was sure she didn't hear.

I had forty dollars to my name when we arrived in Tunica, Mississippi. If a miracle didn't happen, it was going to be a long week for me. When I used to deal on the SunCruz Casino ship, I often faced the Wheel of Fortune machines. If I was watching, someone almost always won. I took this as a sign. As soon as we arrived, I put twenty out of my forty in the Wheel of Fortune machine. On the very first spin, luck was on my side as I hit the bonus wheel. The bonus spun around and landed on one thousand. I just won a cool grand on my first spin. My cash out amount was $1,017. We were not only in the casino industry, but where we came from, it was customary to tip the slot attendants. I wanted to tip a hundred, but my Spidey-Sense went up. I felt Mike wouldn't approve. When I tried to tip the slot attendant $17, Mike still lost his mind. He made quite the scene. Of course, my intuition was right there telling me this was not a good match up, that he was upset and I wouldn't have to rely on him for money that trip. Did I listen? I had no idea what was going on with me. Up to that point, I had met no one else like me. I thought I was delusional.

The thought crossed my mind again that if we had a child, that when she was eighteen, something unimaginable would happen to her, which would make it impossible for Mike and me to ever be together again. My intention was to protect her by praying. I have manifested so much, sure God, Yahweh, would protect me from this tragedy. Believing I was divinely protected in all ways was naïve of me. I was in love. I had never really been in love before. Women are raised so blindly and by Hollywood movies that they truly believe a happy ending is guaranteed. I was certainly one of them.

I also believed that love was enough. Mike and I had been together for two years. Though he never told me he loved me, I could feel it. That was just as good in my book. Mike was a very cranial man, extremely intellectual. It was his intellect that got me to take my clothes off. Remember that video game I played at the bar? Mike answered all the trivia questions on a trivia game correctly for three hours straight, obliterating any previous high score by a mile. I had never seen anything like it. When he watches Jeopardy, he gets ninety-nine out of a hundred questions right. I begged him throughout our relationship to try out for the game show. He wouldn't even think of entertaining the idea. I was so smitten with how smart this man was that it blinded me to serious warning signs.

With the money I won, I had a great time. I sat down at a limit poker game and came in on the big blind. I had suited connectors, like a seven and eight of clubs. There were eight people in for the maximum raise pre-flop. Flops are the three community cards that the dealer lays out on the table in Texas Hold 'Em. I flopped the best straight, and there was no possibility of a flush. What I flopped is also known as the "nuts." The best possible hand in combination with the flop. After the flop, there was another betting round. By the time the action got back to me, the raising was capped. I believe a jack hit the turn. The turn is the next community card the dealer places on the table. I once again checked. Betting went crazy again, and again I made a smooth call.

On the river, the last community card dealt was a king. I checked again. It was once again capped to me. I still had the best hand. It was revealed that one player had a lower straight, while another had acquired a set of jacks on the turn. For those who may be unfamiliar with the term, a set refers to having three of a kind. The same situation occurred on the river where yet another player picked up a set of kings.

As I was raking in the giant pot filled with one-dollar white chips, I found myself unable to contain my laughter and ended up chuckling out loud. A vision of what was about to happen formed in my mind, causing me to giggle uncontrollably.

I asked, "Where are the racks?"

A player chimed in, "Racks? What do you mean racks? You are not leaving, are you?"

I looked at him dead in the eye and said, "You don't really think I am going to sit here and give it back, do you? Thank you, gentlemen, for a quick and pleasant round of poker. I wish you all the best." I racked up and walked away.

Mike and his cronies were playing blackjack, and of course, counting cards. It was a hysterical situation because his friends were making money hand over fist. One was up twenty-nine thousand, the other fifteen thousand, and the third eight thousand dollars. Mike was down fifteen hundred bucks. After two days of these shenanigans, their casino host approached them. She said in a perfect southern drawl, "My bosses say you guys are the best blackjack players they have ever seen. They say you are welcome to play all our games except blackjack." This petite beauty queen of a casino host had us all under such a spell with her beautiful energy that we had to ask her to repeat herself, much to the delight of everyone. Because she was so beautiful, so adorable, and so damn cute, we all started laughing. She had more to say.

"But don't worry, we are still taking you guys to the Grizzly game in our limo in Memphis and, of course, the (whatever the name of the strip joint) afterwards. Also, your suites are still comped."

One boss didn't miss a beat. "I had talked to so and so about taking us to Beale Street tomorrow night."

"Oh, I don't think that will be a problem either."

We were all a little stunned. When she walked away, Mike said, "I must be the only guy in the history of the world banned from playing blackjack while losing. I'm down $1500!" We all busted out laughing again. We knew we were lucky to still be there, to be comped, and we had two days of fun ahead of us! These guys prided themselves on being professional gamblers, and a true professional gambler doesn't just gamble. He finds the best odds, angle, whatever, to beat the system. So, there was no way these guys were going to play slots or anything else. They spent the day shooting pool in their suite. I ate.

We went to the Grizzly basketball game in Memphis in the limo. It was an awesome ride. It was not my first limo ride. On Wednesday nights, me and two other girls went to a nightclub for ladies' night. One of the girls was friendly with this limo driver, who apparently was happy to drive us around. It was quite the scene when we would arrive at the club in our stretch Hummer limo. My life, so strange. The bouncers would usher us straight to the VIP section, where ladies drank for free and we would dance the night away until the limo came back for us a few hours later.

At the Grizzly game, my "delusion"—now my intuition—said, "Pay attention to that player. His name is Pau Gasol. He is from your home country. He is going to be a superstar." I immediately googled him and sure enough, he was a little-known basketball player from Spain.

Pau Gasol would become a superstar and this would not be my first prediction of this type either. Every time I would see Pau Gasol on the news I would hear, "We told you so." Let me be clear, when I say "hear," I really mean feel. My messages come through telepathically through my solar plexus and then I translate them. This process was extremely confusing for a very long time until I read a book that explained it all to me called Opening to Channel. As I read that book, I also had a metaphysical experience that caused everything to fall into place. It was at that moment when I understood how it all worked. Even though it is still cloudy, I am determined to master it in this lifetime, according to my intuition.

Once the Grizzly game had ended, they took us to visit a local gentlemen's club where the dress code required the girls to be in bikinis. Having grown up in South Florida where attending such places was a regular occurrence amongst my friends, we quickly became bored as we were used to seeing the most beautiful naked women. I have the utmost respect for these women because I could never do their jobs. I have a deep appreciation for natural beauty, so I never objected to these types of outings. You don't have to be gay to appreciate a good-looking specimen of the same sex.

Our ride back was filled with boozy chaos as we all laughed and relived what the hostess had said over and over. Mike, still in honest shock that he had been banned while losing, made it all even funnier. It was one of the best times of my life.

The next night we were to meet them on Beale Street for some drinking. Mike was always late for everything. They didn't wait for us, so we took our own car and parked in a parking garage. We met them at a specific bar where the big boss announced he was buying everyone in our group every shot the bartender could think of. A small amount of alcohol is enough to make me intoxicated because of my sensitivity. I looked at Mike in horror. He said, "Just do your best. I'll take care of the rest." Mike was almost six-foot-three. He used to go out drinking with his friends every night, have countless beers, and even take occasional shots without being affected. After the first few shots, I would only taste each one and he took care of what was left. By shot fifteen, I started to realize we may have an issue on our hands. It was going to be one of two times I ever saw Mike drunk. What had we gotten ourselves into? Mike said, "Keep 'em coming, I can take it." His boss, also starting to show signs of inebriation, kept asking the bartender, "What else you got?" in a thick New York accent. These were not the kind of folks you said "no" to.

I think they stopped at twenty or twenty-one. I was the most coherent one of the group. Being the only female with four drunk men made me feel uncomfortable. Mike was fiercely protective of me, always. I trusted the process. It was floated that we would go back with them in the limo. Mike quickly agreed. He mentioned we would come back for the car the next day. It was a strange ride. I kept feeling one of the men having inappropriate thoughts about me. All I kept thinking was, not even if I were single and you were one of the last guys on Earth. He was a good looking second or third generation Italian from an infamous family. He bagged almost every female he turned his attention to. Gross. Not my type.

When we came back from Mississippi, I realized I was ovulating. I said to Mike after we dropped off Adam that if he was to have an accident yesterday, today, or tomorrow, I would get pregnant. I had a moment of weakness. The time we spent together was so amazing. If we needed to have a child to be together, so be it.

CHAPTER 11

Skye

After returning from Tunica, we made plans with Mike's friends at a Flannigan's because he was desperate to share what happened on our trip. At Flannigan's I went to the ladies' room where Mike followed me in. He was extremely rough with me and had "an accident." He left as soon as he came, no pun intended. When I was washing my hands, I felt a sensation I have never felt before or after. I also knew instantly I was pregnant. I started counting out the days. As soon as day twenty-one hit, I got an over-the-counter early pregnancy test just to confirm what I already knew. I desired to give the man I loved deeply what he wanted. I was so excited for him, for us. The feeling of excitement was overwhelming as I thought about showing him. The early pregnancy test confirmed it.

Initially, he was very excited. But it wasn't long after that he started saying awful things like a child doesn't need two parents and questioning the authenticity of my pregnancy. He believed in the possibility that I was making it up to manipulate him into being with me. I didn't want another child. I was doing this for him. My heart was broken. We went through another period of break-ups. He was hesitant at first, but after my persistent pleading, he finally agreed to come with me to an ultrasound so we could discover the sex of our baby. This man, in my opinion, honestly believed until that moment that I was deceiving him.

After he saw the baby on the ultrasound and found she was a girl, everything changed. He became a doting partner. I felt an immense sense of relief and silently thanked my lucky stars that it was finally over.

My two other girl's names were Sabrina and Savannah. I wanted to find a name that started with an S. I do everything by feeling and I was feeling a Dutch name. When I looked up Dutch names that start with 'S' on Google, Skye was the first name to come up. I knew instantly that was her name, absolutely not remembering what I was told on the playground when I was nine. I told Mike I had the perfect name, Skye, because I loved looking at the sky so much. He loved it too, and it was done. We were decided.

Around the same time, I lost both my jobs. One employer laid me off after discovering my pregnancy, while the other terminated me on grounds of suspicion of dealing at a private game. Afterwards, I started playing for a living. I had no other choice. I was using some of my supernatural abilities, but I honestly thought everyone had them. My request to God was that I be blessed with the opportunity to earn fifteen hundred dollars each week. The total amount earned from live poker and tournaments combined was precisely fifteen hundred per week. Depending on how well I was running, it could take anywhere from a few hours to sixty or seventy hours to reach my goal during certain weeks. The long weeks were not fun.

My exceptional performance in tournaments led me to getting a sponsor who offered me the sweetest deal in the poker world, making it difficult to say no. The arrangement I made with him was that he would provide all the money for the tournaments, and in return, I agreed to give him half of whatever I won, along with the entry ticket. If I busted out, I was not liable for anything. His horse started paying off. I was making money for him every week. Mike arranged the first one thousand-dollar buy-in, multi table tournament in South Florida on the new St. Tropez Casino ship. The St. Tropez was a reincarnation of the old ship he used to work on, The Seascape. There were some irregularities with the Seascape. The St. Tropez was born after a new boat was purchased. Mike was fortunate enough to work as a casino host and Poker Tournament Director, having earned his place as one of the "trusted" boys thanks to his shot drinking in Tunica.

As was often the case, I was outlasting the player field in the thousand-dollar tourney. When we got down to three players, it was me against two identical twins. I thought, "Is this a joke?" as I looked around for the hidden camera. The Universe has a sense of humor. Since negotiating on the final table was one of my strengths, I started doing it right away. I had already been told by the Universe that I would never come in first in a multi table tournament, when I would ask why, I was told, "Because your life is going so incredible, this is one of the highlights of their lives." Insert eye roll. I was like, ok, we will see.

Despite being severely out-chipped, I managed to convince the twins to agree to my proposals by continually moving money down from first to second and third place. Poker tables are all about survival of the fittest, but in the end, players share great camaraderie.

At one point, I had no choice. I was on the big blind, which means I already had chips in the game. A pair of sixes, also known as "pocket sixes" is what I had when I looked down at my starting hand. It was the best hand I had seen at the final table since I got there. I went all in. I got called instantly by the button, who was slow playing pocket aces. Slow playing means he did not raise his hand, he just called the standard bet. The flop came ace, six. We both flopped three of a kind. The dealer and I locked eyes because we both felt it at the same time. We both knew in that instant that the next card was a six. She later told me after the game was over how she felt the six coming. I won the hand with four sixes over his aces full of sixes. This hand helped me secure second place. I won like fifteen or eighteen thousand dollars. My sponsor was pleased. He had clearly chosen the right horse.

It was around this time that I caught the eye of Michael Mizrachi, who would become a world-famous poker player. We worked together at the Seminoles, and he was also one of the few seeking to be an excellent dealer. There were a few of us that took pride in what we did. Mike and I had an attraction towards each other that transcended this realm. I now believe that it is a past life connection. We admired and followed each other's play.

Skye's pregnancy had been fairly pleasant. My ribs were acting strange as the baby had limited space. I was induced on August fifth. It was a strange event. People just kept showing up. If you know anything about me, it is that I like privacy. Bless her, Sabrina was going to be there for the birth, along with Mike's sister and my parents. A friend of mine would also be there as well as Paul, Mike's best friend, and my father-in-law. That is when I opted for the epidural. There was so much energy in that room, I needed a break. My labor was over eighteen hours, my longest ever by nine hours. I was so surprised when I got the epidural that the divine energy didn't show up. I really considered the possibility of it being a side effect of the epidural, but it wasn't.

My OB-GYN arrived while I was napping and woke me up to tell me it was time to push. It only took one push. The delivery was absolutely painless for me. Skye was born with a white veil. Sabrina and I looked at each other, horrified. She looked like a corpse. I felt a shiver run through me as if it was some sort of foreshadowing. I thought I was being ridiculous. Like with all my children, it was love at first sight. Who knows what went wrong during my first delivery, but the Universe made up for it and the others were easy. My intuition told me my OB-GYN would feel bad charging me and a few hours later she said exactly that.

Skye's room had the most beautiful fairies for decorations. I put so much love into her room that some people could feel it when they walked in.

Until I gave birth, I was successfully keeping everything going. Under the agreement that he would contribute towards the mortgage, my first husband Daniel moved into my four-bedroom home. The agreement was that he would pay seven hundred dollars out of the total fifteen-hundred-dollar mortgage. The remaining amount was paid by me as an informal child support arrangement, away from the official records, because the kids were with him during the week. Our divorce agreement stated that we had joint custody. He threatened me to not even think about filing for full custody. I was terrified of this man. The opportunity provided me with the chance to have my children close by and have regular access to them. Daniel never made a single payment. After seven or eight months, I had to evict him as I had to sell the house because I couldn't keep it all together anymore. I sold the house to Mike. We kept our finances separate.

Since he was the father of my child, I only asked for twenty thousand more than I originally paid for it, though it was worth a lot more.

As soon as he bought the house, he put it up for rent. He found a tenant willing to pay twenty-five hundred dollars per month. He was ecstatic with his investment, and even more so a couple of years later when he could double his money.

I kept playing poker after Skye was born at a home game. It was the best place to make money in town. This couple became the owners of the game after its original owner sold it. Dennis, a wealthy, older southern gentleman, was not only an excellent Omaha High Low Poker player, but he was also an outstanding teacher. He taught me many valuable things about the game. We were friendly. Dennis once took me out to Ruth Chris's for a date and shopping at Victoria's Secret afterwards. Dennis presented me with an indecent proposal. He suggested taking me out three or four times a week, saying that nights like the one we just had could become my lifestyle. In exchange, he would pay all my bills. I wouldn't have to work anymore. I understood what "taking me out meant". It's just not my thing. I believe in love. Furthermore, he was married. Once I declined his offer, he quickly approached another poker dealer who was more than willing to accept the same deal and who took advantage of him as much as possible. She stopped working. She would come to the game with her Louis Vuitton bags.

I don't like labels of any kind, they are divisive. One thing is to own such a bag because you find them to be beautiful, but most own these bags so they can make other women feel less than or give themselves an ego boost because of their insecurities. I would love to ask the women who carry these bags the following questions: Why would you ever want another being to feel bad when they realize they can't afford a bag like that? Why would you walk around with a bag worth hundreds, if not thousands, of dollars? Aren't you afraid of getting mugged? If you break or stain it, wouldn't you have preferred if that money had gone to someone who is in need?

Our first Christmas together, Mike bought me a Christian Dior purse I thought I really wanted. I did not enjoy the experience. To minimize my impact on the environment, I've started using washable purses. I believe I have had my current day purse for four years and it still looks great. I do have one "going out" purse made out of tooled leather, which I love. It is also my concealed carry bag.

The game was sold to Dennis and his new girlfriend. With some clever manipulation, she was able to get him to buy her not only a Mercedes, but also a home. I meet people every day who are in relationships where they are physically, mentally, and or financially abused. Many stay because of the "in sickness and in health, good and bad" promises they made, sacrificing years of happiness so they can feel they are doing the right thing. They stay to make someone else happy. Some people choose to remain in their current situation because of their fear of not being accepted by someone new. Thinking to themselves, "Who else would put up with me?" God wants you to have the best experience possible here on Earth. A fulfilling love relationship can be part of that. Staying in these situations as a martyr does not earn you any extra points in Heaven.

Dennis and his girlfriend were breaking up when Skye was just a few months old. During this, Dennis let everyone know that the game would be shut down. My immediate reaction to the situation was to panic. This is where I made my living. I brought up the idea with Mike that we should take over the game. I started negotiations after he expressed interest. Dennis wanted to punish his girl by destroying the game. Another friend of Dennis, who made a living from the game, was Mark, a local real estate agent.

It was the only angle I had. In order to persuade Dennis to allow the game to continue, I promised him I would teach his best friend, Mark, how to become a poker dealer. Mark was one of the first open gay men I met. He made it seem so normal that it didn't bother anyone who knew him. He was also blessed with beautiful parents who accepted him and probably knew before he did. They later told me they had their first real suspicions when they found magazines featuring good looking males under his mattress. Mark and I got along extremely well. Dennis finally relented.

We moved locations. We placed our home game next to a Subway shop. Mike had a great reputation as Mr. Transparency. Folks trusted us immediately and with good reason. We gave them a catered lunch or dinner, and Mark often made his famous tuna salad for snack and served drinks to all who wanted one. We didn't serve alcohol. I could still make a living. We prided ourselves on delivering a game that was on the "up and up."

Our home game was running for approximately six months. I was not present one day, which was uncommon. I was working twelve hours a day, six days a week. Two guys from New York walked in and tried to shake Mike down. They wanted fifteen hundred dollars a week in protection money. By some weird coincidence, the cousin of Mike's good friend had sold his bar to a local mafia boss who was released from prison a year or two earlier. Mike immediately requested a meeting. The mafia boss and his associates offered to handle it, and since we were close, they only asked for a small taste in return.

They arranged for a sit down with the guys from New York. We never heard another word from them. The small taste was really small. Mike explained that the fifty a week was more of a gesture of respect than a monetary contribution. Despite his intimidating nickname, Johnny "Killer," the courier, was always courteous and polite. We always invited him to stay for a meal, which he always accepted. I would chuckle at the thought that a mafia guy was eating dinner with us. My life, so weird.

It was around this time when I attended my first out-of-state poker tournament in Foxwoods, Connecticut. I was going to be there on my birthday. When Mike and I first met, we made an agreement to take vacations by ourselves from time to time. Did I mention I love solitude? I'm the person who goes to the movies or a restaurant by herself. I have always believed that one should not let the fear of being alone stop them from exploring the world, which is why I have even gone on a cruise all by myself. I'm very content with my own company. Perhaps I became accustomed to not having friends due to my weird circumstances. If you are friends with me, the dark-side will always find a way in, unless you are an incarnated angel.

After taking a flight to New York, I rented a car and drove to Foxwoods where I stayed at a nearby bed-and-breakfast. It was also the first time I would sleep on a memory foam mattress, and I was smitten. I slept so amazingly well that when I got back home I knew I needed one.

The tournaments were a little different from what I was used to. You were allowed to reenter, which I thought was absurd. How could you really determine who the best player is if you can enter as many times as you want? I didn't let that deter me. Despite playing excellent poker, I kept having bad luck that led to frustration and tears in the bathroom. The next day was my birthday. I started my birthday by waking up early and playing some slots before the tournament later that day. Every slot machine I touched, I won on. I finally asked myself, "is this a birthday blessing?" It was my first time experiencing something like this. Through telepathy, I was informed that this was a gift from the Native American spirits that rule this area. Insert eye roll. My Akashic Records will reflect that I rolled my eyes at the time I heard this, but also started blushing a little as I felt it was true. If Akashic Records are real, as I understand them, they contain a comprehensive record of every thought and spoken word ever uttered by an individual. I'm sure a "yeah right" escaped my mouth. "Here we go with that delusion again."

The fact was that I couldn't lose. I tried. It wasn't happening. I walked out with over five thousand dollars in winnings. Unfortunately, I missed out on the tournament. I couldn't believe what was happening! In the evening, I went to play live poker. I sat down at a ten-twenty limit Texas Hold'Em game where I got hit with the deck. I noticed that every single hand I folded was a winner. For a dozen hands in a row. Eventually, I played any two cards. I won the next six hands in a row and walked away with over three thousand dollars. I guess the birthday celebration continued at the Poker table.

My whole life, strange things have happened to me. I'm forty-six as I write this. For the first forty-two years, I didn't believe it, but hoped that if it were true, it would manifest someday. Knowing this was a possibility since I was little has made for a very long life. It has felt like I'm waiting out a prison sentence waiting for my life to start. As I write this, I'm still waiting and working on myself in the meantime. He who conquers himself is the mightiest warrior, as Confucius said. It is two steps forward and one step back. Or, like a spiritual mentor said, three steps forward and two steps back. My dream is to lead a spiritual life and help others who desire the same. If someday, in some way, I can truly help mankind, my knees would hit the ground in humility. One of the greatest honors on Earth is to help others. However, it's important to avoid being taken advantage of.

Mike Mizrachi was there at the same tournament in Connecticut. He was elated. He had won an astounding amount, over eighty thousand dollars, playing live poker. During several tournaments, I had the pleasure of pointing out a talented young player named Michael Mizrachi. I confidently told others to keep an eye on him, as he was destined for greatness before he told me about his windfall. Six months later, Mike won The Commerce Casino main event tournament for one point two million dollars and made national news. As I reflect on the advice I gave him, I now recognize that it was actually a message from my intuition: "never indulge in blackjack or any casino games, and you will undoubtedly emerge as one of the most successful poker players in history." My future roommate accompanied him to his first roulette game. She said Mike lost more money than we could make in six months.

My trip was a success, but I felt guilty for not winning any tournaments, so I split the entry fees of the poker tournaments with my sponsor. I realized that playing poker professionally was not for me. The stress of having to perform well was getting to me.

CHAPTER 12

The Kingdom of God

Mike had taken a weekend trip to Biloxi with some of his friends. They had made a mistake in his casino rating. When he was in his room one night, he got a phone call from a casino host.

"Mr. Litvin, I see here you had a bit of a rough night. It shows you lost fifty thousand dollars, is that correct?" Mike, having been a casino host, didn't miss a beat. He said, "Yeah, my wife is going to kill me." He had, in fact, only lost five hundred dollars. As a result, we were flown regularly to Biloxi. We were even given a ten-day, two-suites stay during a hurricane evacuation once, as well as many stays in Las Vegas.

Our home game kept flourishing, so we had to add a third table. We had a player who was constantly recruiting for us. He did this all on his own. He was a natural salesperson. Because of all the business he brought in, we bought him into our weekly tournament as a reward. Give them an inch and they'll take a mile. Over time, he was not satisfied with us buying him into our tournament and wanted more. What no one knew about this game is that we had a silent partner. Someone who no one could know about or our game would be destroyed. She was basically extorting us for silence. It was Dennis's ex girl. She had threatened to shut us down way before any mafiosos had ever shown up. Bringing on this new guy was going to present some serious issues. Our silent partner wouldn't hear of it. Despite me telling her he brought in a

97

lot of business she still demanded an ungodly amount of money from him upfront. I knew that would be a no go for him. He eventually started his own home game.

There was a buy-in limit of three hundred dollars for our home game, but players could re-buy as many times as they wished. This kept the game fair and open to many. Having a lot of cash just lying around is never a smart move. That was a lot of heat. At the start, a group of Middle Eastern men began playing with us. Because of their deep pockets, they were not satisfied with the buy-in. When I explained that the buy-in limit was for security reasons, they laughed at me.

We kept butting heads because they couldn't handle a woman as an authority figure. They told Mike to send me to a school for Middle Eastern women in Orlando so that I would come back with my head bowed down. The next time I saw them I said, "When I find the man that keeps me at home safely with my children, that is the day I will not only bow my head to that man but I will make sure he is completely satisfied every night. I just haven't found the man." I meant it and they could feel that I meant it. That shut them up.

These men went on to start their own game. They were robbed at gunpoint twice and unable to call the authorities. The robbers allegedly stole a sum of one hundred and twenty thousand dollars the first time. That did not stop those guys from playing. They kept going for a long time. Allegedly, the FBI was investigating one of them. During the investigation, they identified additional individuals of concern at the game; folks who were wanted by agencies like the Interpol and CIA.

Our recruiter started his own game with a young man as a partner. We were out at a Thanksgiving get together when I received a phone call. The Hollywood Police department had busted the recruiter's game. My spirit guides warned me that the guys were going to rat us out, that it was over. I told Mike. He disagreed. I immediately told him I was done.

Mike and I had gone on our first cruise together a few weeks prior to that. Paul, his best friend, was getting married. It has come to my attention that strange things tend to happen to me during voyages, especially if I'm near or on water. Not only was this my first cruise, but I had also booked my first professional massage. My appointment was at nine in the morning and I arrived on time. I'm always on time. Being late is something that I cannot tolerate since it shows a lack of respect for other people's time.

As soon as the door opened, I was struck by the sight of the massage therapist who walked in. I couldn't help but think he was the most handsome human being I had seen until that moment. He may have also felt the same way because it felt like I was feeling someone else's arousal. As I am sensitive to other people's arousal, it can affect me as well. Therefore, I made a conscious effort to focus on my breathing in order to avoid becoming aroused, which I felt was a sign of disrespect towards my partner at the time. As the arousal kept building, I found myself gripping the sheets tightly. I was doing my absolute best to focus on my breathing, but suddenly, to my surprise, I found myself floating up on the ceiling of the massage suite. I saw myself lying on the massage table while receiving a massage. The endless ocean's vastness was all I could see when I looked to the right. When I looked to the left, I saw the same thing. It was breathtaking, literally. Fearing a panic attack, I chose to stay with my physical body. When the massage was over, the therapist said "Ok, we are done." In an instant, my consciousness was pulled back into my physical form.

I told the guy, "I just had an out-of-body experience." He was more than happy to talk about it. People always thought I was crazy or lying. I was so tired of it, I shut him down without hesitation. Also, how could I explain I had an out-of-body experience trying to prevent arousal? My life, so weird.

The groom organized an excursion for all the groomsmen in Saint Martin. Mike was one of the members included in the group who went sailing together. Being born with a fearless spirit, I set off to explore on my own. I disembarked from the cruise ship. I found myself in the busy shopping district in downtown Saint Martin on the Dutch side.

Since Mike had won a jackpot of over twenty-five thousand at the casino, I had a few thousand dollars on me. It still amazes me that folks are constantly winning prizes around me. His recurrent complaint since the day we met was that he couldn't win a jackpot. He must have repeated it countless times, which made me pray for it to happen.

On a night after work, I met Mike at the Hard Rock Casino. Mike had been there for hours, gambling with his friends. He was upset because he had no more cash on him. He wanted to leave. As soon as I saw the newly installed Cleopatra slot machines, I knew I wanted to stay. I gave him a hundred bucks. He went off to play a slot machine of his own. When I was done with the new game, I went to play another favorite slot machine of mine. While there, I got a text from Mike. "You better get over here. They are about to throw me out."

"What, where are you?" I asked.

"I'm over by the dime slot machines."

When I approached, I noticed a slot attendant standing next to him, and a blue screen displayed on his monitor. I had a strong feeling he was kidding. I was relieved to find out he was indeed joking around. No one was getting thrown out.

At first, I thought he won twenty-five hundred. When I realized it was twenty-five thousand, I had an unexpected reaction. I screamed! Now I understand why people scream at casinos. It was crucial that I had that experience in order to avoid being judgmental towards others. I used to think that those people were just trying to be the center of attention. I realized then it was an involuntary reaction. My apologies, Universe. The Kingdom of God is all around you and always teaching you. Lesson learned. Mike made it crystal clear that he was going to keep all the winnings from the slot machine, although I gave him the money to play. He could see the sincerity in my eyes as I explained that I would have split the money with him if I had won, regardless of whose money it was. After changing his mind, he gave me four thousand dollars.

I got tired of shopping around Saint Martin. I spotted a local casino and thought playing slots would be an easy way to kill some time. While waiting for the waitress to bring me my Coca-Cola, I had a clairaudient experience. "There is something wrong with your drink."

"OMG, here we go with this delusion again." I rolled my eyes. When the drink arrived, I sniffed it. I have a super sensory sense of smell as well. It didn't smell right. I can even smell germs. I took a very slow sip. I only allowed the liquid to touch my lips and the tip of my tongue. As soon as the liquid touched my lips and the tip of my mouth, the room started spinning. To make sure the drink wasn't served to anyone else, I put my cigarette out in the drink. Then I heard, "Good, we will tell you when it is safe to go."

I sat there in a state of shock. I couldn't believe the room had just spun. Despite playing the slot machine, the sensation of being watched consumed my mind. The specific amount won or lost was not clear to me. I set the slot machine on a small bet. I was just going through the motions. Also, I didn't know how long I was going to be there. After more than two hours, I heard clairaudiently again, "They have lost interest. You may go now." My heart pounding, I hurried back to the ship, eager to tell Mike about what had just happened. It was a blow to my self-esteem when he didn't take my word for it. He didn't believe me. He accused me of seeking attention because he had left me alone all day. There was little I could do, since he did not have confidence in my abilities.

The day after his home game was busted, the recruiter called me. As I picked up the phone, I heard telepathically, "This phone call is being listened to by the FBI. Please trust what is about to happen." Something started speaking through me and I gave the performance of a lifetime. Despite the circumstances, I remained calm as I delivered every word with the right connotation.

For quite a while, I stayed away from the home game. I took my intuition's advice seriously. I was done. The tournament had been facing difficulties ever since the other game was busted. One night, Mike unexpectedly sold out the home game poker tournament and they were short a dealer. This led to a big drama. I was asked to fill in. Despite my reluctance, I agreed to the proposition, as I had been home bored for weeks. As Mike parked the car, my attention was drawn towards two young white guys who were sitting in the window of the Subway. As I gazed at them, a dark, unsettling feeling crept in. The Universe was about to put on a show.

A full house of thirty-one players on three tables is what I encountered. It was mayhem. I ran a much smoother operation, but I was no longer in charge. The tournament was maybe fifteen minutes under way when I heard the outside door click. I knew Mike had gone out to smoke a cigarette, and it was unusual for him to let the door click.

A few moments had passed when suddenly we were jolted by the sound of the loudest knock I had ever heard. I thought we were being robbed. I sprang into action and leaped to the opposite end of the table. From there, I instructed everyone to remain calm and to avoid unlocking any doors. Everyone except one player listened to me.

He opened the back door. If humans only listened to me. They came in guns drawn, dressed in plain clothes, no badges. The guys that had creeped up to Mike by the front door donned the same type of attire. I started asking for identification to make sure we weren't getting robbed. That was when they produced their badges. I never saw a search warrant.

Once we realized it was the police, we were all relieved. The police questioned everyone present and asked for their identification, except me. Mike was extremely brave and stood up and said, "I'm in charge here. I'm the one you want to talk to." He was always very keen on protecting me. Honestly, I hadn't been part of that game for a while when this happened. I stood in the same spot for several hours, observing everything that was going on around me. Then finally one officer looked up at me and asked, "What are you still doing here?"

"Me? I was just leaving," was my response. I bolted for the door. Knowing all the weirdness I had already encountered, I was sure that not being questioned or being in trouble was due to it. Once again, what I perceive to be divine energy surrounded me.

After I left, I got organized and figured out how to get Mike out of jail. It was going to be five hundred dollars to get him out, and it couldn't be done until the morning. I couldn't sleep a wink. It was common knowledge amongst all our players that the funds in the jackpot fund would be used for defense, should it ever come to that. As if it was meant to be, we were led to a specific defense attorney and, coincidentally, his fee aligned perfectly with the exact amount that was saved in the jackpot fund. Which I took as a sign from the Kingdom of God, as I now realize that is how the Kingdom of God truly works for me.

I was brought up with no spirituality, no guiding compass. I was left to figure that out all on my own. My beliefs are my own, as I believe spirituality is individual. It is possible that at some point in the future, my perspective on this may shift, but as of now, this is how my spirituality manifests.

He was initially charged with a felony. I would hear telepathically, "Everything is going to end well." Only a fraction of the items and money that were confiscated showed up on the evidence list. This only made us more afraid. Would the police now follow us around to shut us up? We knew the truth about what should have been on that evidence list. It was a scary time.

Mike was in a foul mood all the time after the game ended. We had sold the home we remodeled for way more money than we ever dreamed of and bought a house out West where the schools were better for Skye. Our new home was a dream come true. In-ground pool, four bedrooms, and a big kitchen, which was a shame because I didn't cook yet. We were very happy in this home, but our mortgage was a lot. We had no income, and Mike couldn't get any casino work until his case got resolved.

His defense attorney had advised him to keep asking for continuances, advising that was the best strategy. So that is what we did. It was a strange time in the poker industry, and no one in South Florida was hiring poker dealers. Mike's cousin whom he had gone to poker dealer school with worked for the WSOP, World Series of Poker, and the EPT, European Poker Tour. He traveled the world either dealing or directing poker tournaments. I called him. "Yes, we need dealers for the Harrah's Rincon WSOP Circuit Event. Book a flight and I will let the dealer coordinator know you are coming."

CHAPTER 13

Here Comes the Royal

The World Series of Poker Circuit event consisted of several poker tournaments, with the main event being a ten thousand dollar buy into the tournament, which was the final tournament in the series. I arrived in San Diego and took a very expensive cab ride to Harrah's Rincon in Temecula, California. The flight, being last minute, was expensive. I was informed upon arrival that a shared room would cost twenty-nine dollars per night. It was a ten-day event.

Soon after I arrived, it started raining. This seems to be a common occurrence when I go places. Nonetheless, much needed rain had unexpectedly arrived in southern California. So much so that the torrential rains caused many rockslides and landslides, making the roads difficult to travel on. The result of this was a turnout that was much less than expected. Therefore, there was plenty of spare time, leading dealers to connect and create meaningful relationships. We shared meals and time in the jacuzzi. My roommate was a black male; I didn't bat an eye.

Did I mention I don't have a racist bone in my body? I was actually the only white dealer who would hang out with the clique of black dealers. My perception of the world is not influenced by the color of people's skin. I had a friend who was black for many years, but it only occurred to me she was black after someone mentioned it.

Mike had a roommate when we met. Despite her constant meanness towards me, my heart went out to her because various genetic illnesses afflicted her. I would remind myself that her behavior was a result of her medical issues. My heart still goes out to people like that, but I no longer allow mean people in my life. Setting boundaries is something I had to learn. As is typical with those who receive my blessing, she had a good life. She went to acting school and became a regular dealer at the World Series of Poker and for the World Poker Tour. She dealt many final tables. She traveled to many foreign countries. She even took part in a few Hollywood movies. I was honestly happy for her, however the thought of dealing a final table someday myself did cross my mind. I was selected to deal the final table at this event, she wasn't. Even though she dealt many, I knew she wasn't happy that I was dealing the final and not her. That is where I differ from most humans. I'm always rooting for you.

The final table for this event dragged on and on and became the second longest final table in the history of the WSOP. It was so much so that I had to change my flight going back. Three hours before the end, I had a vision that I would be the last dealer and end it. I even went up to the guy running the final table and said to him, "If you let me in the dealer box, I will finish this up for you." I had to wait for my turn. We were on a six-dealer rotation. Each dealer dealt for thirty minutes. After another two and a half hours, it was my turn again. There were two players left: Prahlad Friedman, recent internet poker sensation, and Chris "Jesus" Ferguson.

The hand that ultimately determined the end of the series began with Prahlad Friedman being dealt a king and a jack, KJ. Chris Ferguson received an ace and a six, or A6. The flop came JAA. Prahlad flopped two pairs while Chris made three aces. Chris raises Prahlad's bet, pretending to bluff him out of the game by leveraging his position. Prahlad calls and the next card, the turn, is also an ace. The community cards they share are JAAA. Prahlad has a full house, aces over jacks, while Jesus has four aces. On the river came a king, JAAAK. Prahlad, improving his full house, is now in a situation he can't get out of. Chris goes all-in, Prahlad reluctantly calls to find out that Chris was indeed holding the fourth ace. This left Prahlad beyond crippled and within a few hands, the tournament was over. Just like in my vision. I was more stunned about the paranormal experience I was having than anything else. If you see my face on the ESPN's video, I am white as a ghost! Little did I know of all that was yet to come!

My trip to California was so enjoyable that, even though I broke even after paying for my flight, accommodation, transportation, and food expenses, I immediately made arrangements for the next event. The next event started a month later. Mike and I were having real problems. He was extremely jealous that I got to deal poker on TV. Seeing my children finally understand what I do for a living was an extremely cool experience for me. One would assume that he would be proud of my achievements, however, he was out of his mind with jealousy. He kept accusing me of flirting with Jesus. Of course, I had a conversation with Chris Ferguson. I accompanied him during his ESPN interview and we talked extensively about poker. I was trying to earn a tip. This tip I was to share with my fellow dealers, so I had a duty to hustle. If it were just my tip, I would have stayed quiet. I really don't care about money. It is a blessing and a curse. Trusting that God will provide for me has always been my belief. It's a blessing because when you don't care about money, you absolutely do not worry about it. On the other hand, I would have a lot more money if I cared enough to care about it.

Mike and I had broken up by the time I went to the next event in Las Vegas. My love for him was so intense that I couldn't find interest in anyone else. I was driving to Las Vegas because I was going to deal several poker events, including the World Series of Poker. I would be there for several months. Mike didn't truly believe that I was going to leave. He was stunned to see my van pull out of the driveway.

Upon arriving in Las Vegas, I decided that on my first day I would spend my time indulging in video poker. I hit an abnormal number of royal flushes, which is the best possible hand. I hit five different times. Most people are lucky to hit five times in a lifetime. Of course, in the back of my head, I was wondering if it had something to do with all the weirdness I had encountered throughout my life. Whenever I do something for the first time, the Universe tries to make it special for me.

I dealt the first event, which culminated with a fifty thousand dollar buy in, multi table tournament. The money was terrible. I hadn't seen wages that low since I dealt quarter and fifty cent games.

I made it a habit to visit the initial casino daily, the one where I got fortunate enough to get five royal flushes. I would deposit twenty dollars into a video poker machine bank that was connected to other machines, creating a substantial jackpot. The jackpot was close to four thousand dollars when I started this routine. I could eat at their buffet every day because I had a lot of comp dollars. You earn comp dollars by using your player's card, either by inserting it into a slot machine or presenting it to a dealer while playing. You can then spend these dollars on food, accommodations, and, at some casinos, on-site shops. I kept this up for six weeks, but one day I couldn't put in twenty dollars. Low pay and sending money back home had left me low on funds. I went to work. It was going to be yet another slow night. Naturally, I made friends with the only black dealer. I was glad to help him improve his dealing skills. We became best work buddies. "I'm bored. I really want to get out of here," he said that day. During our conversation, I mentioned to him my afternoon routine of playing the same poker machines. I also shared that I was broke and therefore unable to put in my daily twenty. I was sure the jackpot was getting ready to hit. It was over eight thousand now. He said, "I have money, let's go."

We got to Terrible's Casino. Yes, that really was the name. We sat at machines next to each other. He put forty into my machine and forty in his. He lost his money after a little while. I had exactly eighty dollars, so I asked him, "Should I cash out?" I absolutely didn't want him to lose his money. He said "No play on." As soon as he said that, I hit the button. I was dealt the royal flush. It was worth $8334. We were both in shock. I did not scream this time.

We started discussing money. Of course, I told him it was his money. Despite my doubts, he vehemently insisted that the money he gave me was mine and that it was not his. Then I said, "You will take at least half then."

"Absolutely not. You have to pay taxes on that money. If you give me two thousand, I will be over the moon".

The thought that crossed my mind next was, "Is he going to try to get into my pants?" I immediately felt concerned. This man was a total and complete gentleman. He never acted inappropriately with me or even tried to kiss me, touch me, or anything else. A truly excellent human being.

Mike called me on one of my days off. He was terrified because he was convinced a black Mercedes was following him. The game was busted around the same time the mafia boss protecting it was caught. Mike was worried they thought he had snitched, which we would never do. Mike and I believed in being "stand up" people. Always do the right thing and betray no one. It was our code of honor. When all else is stripped away, your dignity, honor, and pride remain as the only tangible remnants of your existence on Earth. Those are the possessions that will accompany you into the afterlife, not your wealth and material belongings.

Mike had something very important to share with me. "I should have told you this a long time ago. I'm sorry I didn't say it sooner. I love you." We made plans for him to come and visit. We were still on the MGM welfare plan, the comps that Mike earned by being a "fifty thousand dollar" loser. We stayed at the MGM and went to the Bernard Hopkins versus Jermain Taylor boxing match. Afterwards, we had reservations at Craftsteak, MGM's premier steakhouse. It was a surreal experience as we walked by the many celebrities and others who were standing in line waiting to get in. We got seated for our free meals. This is how it works when you are in God's army, you are rewarded in unexpected ways.

I was so in love with this man that I put up with things I would never put up with. Like him not telling me he loved me for four years, or freaking out when I had professional success. I was under the illusion and delusion that love was enough to make a marriage work. All I wanted in life was to be his wife and to love him for the rest of my life.

Yahweh always has me witness things. The dealers at World Series of Poker that year didn't receive any gratuities. All they received was their usual salary and cut from the tournaments after the tips were stolen. Apparently, there was an investigation, but nothing ever came of it. Looking back on that time, I realize how young and inexperienced I was. If the same situation were to happen today, there is no way I would tolerate it.

The summer in Las Vegas was not very profitable. After weighing my options, I made the choice to go back to my home in Florida. Even though I had been given great job offers in both Las Vegas and California, Mike was so against it that I couldn't consider taking them. My intuition was disappointed, but I made the decision to go against it and go back. I could feel it was the wrong choice.

As soon as I got back, I got a job at Dania Jai Alai. Dania Jai Alai was a place where the game of Jai Alai was played and wagers could be placed on the players of that game. Also known as a parimutuel, you could also place bets on horse races across the world. As a gambling house, they were allowed to have a poker room. About a month had passed since I returned to my hometown when I found out that the tournament I dealt in California had made it onto ESPN. I received a lot of admiration from players and dealers alike. There were two people who were extremely unhappy with my television debut: Mike and my new boss.

People should always be wary of those who want to be in charge. Throughout my career, I have encountered numerous bosses who were plagued by ego and insecurity issues, resulting in their desire to be the boss in order to bolster their own sense of self-worth. These are exactly the people who shouldn't be in charge. The fact that I was on TV and being approached by players with compliments about being a celebrity dealer made my boss extremely jealous. One day, he took out a thick binder and instructed me to sit at an empty table in the middle of the Poker Room, where all the guests could see me.

I was caught off guard when this man instructed me to sit at that spot for the entire shift. He told me to read through the binder because he believed I had no understanding of the poker rules. This was perplexing, as I had very little interaction with him before. Most of the guests and dealers were as stunned as I was. Not only was I a textbook perfect dealer, but I was well regarded for my poker knowledge and skills. I had been offered supervisor positions on the regular. I knew the book forwards and backwards. If I find myself intrigued by a certain topic, I make it a point to delve into every aspect and learn everything there is to know about it. That is when my "delusion", now my intuition, came on to tell me that this man was misguided. That this was a one time incident. That he would return to normal after this. Come to think of it, I had a few strange experiences while working there.

A former work friend of mine from the SunCruz ship, worked at Dania Jai Alai for years before I ever worked there. His name was Mr. Kim. He was an older Asian man who had spent most of his life as a cruise ship bartender on one of the major cruise lines. He was a terrible dealer. No one cared. We found his personality so charming that we believed he would be an ideal addition to our team. Mr. Kim, in his broken English, used to call me Cristana. Mr. Kim passed away a few years before I started working at Dania Jai Alai. Throughout my entire time working at Dania Jai Alai, the name that appeared on the schedule every day was Cristana.

The 6th of June in the year 2006 marked another peculiar event. I dealt 666 on the flop several times, either three or four times. The odds of that are astronomical. Also, my paychecks consistently ended with 666 for years at different jobs.

We were lucky enough to go on a cruise to the stunning and famous Panama Canal. The journey lasted ten days. Mike didn't believe me when I confided in him about my supernatural abilities. At twenty-nine, I never shared a prediction with anyone prior to it happening. I always just let it happen and then maybe say, "I knew that was going to happen."

I had a dream during the night that was just like the one I had before with the girl who had long black hair. It was also similar to the dream where I saw the winning lotto numbers. In the dream, I won a jackpot of $1252.34 on a video poker slot machine. The thought crossed my mind about whether I should say something. The answer was "Yes, for once in your life say something." Fine.

"Mike, I'm going to hit a jackpot on a video poker machine for $1252.34, alright? Remember this number, 1252.34." While we were in the Panama Canal, we planned to do our usual routine of renting a car and getting lost for a while in local ports. I love exploring. Going to new places and experiencing different energies and sights brings me an immense amount of joy and happiness. In that specific port, the rule was that passengers could not disembark from the ship unless they had reserved an excursion beforehand. As we had not booked an excursion, we were staying on the ship. Mike drank Diet Coke the way most people drink water. He suggested checking the casino bar to see if they had Diet

Coke. We were surprised to find the casino open, but then it made sense if some guests were not allowed to get off the ship. He got his Diet Coke. As I turned around, to my amazement, there was the machine that I had been dreaming about. One problem, there was a lady playing it.

"I am going to play the machine next to her," I informed Mike before putting in a twenty-dollar bill. It dealt me four deuces, four twos, that paid two hundred and fifty dollars. I cashed it out. We were surprised that the payout was in quarters. That was a lot of quarters. It filled several buckets. That took a hot minute. Then we had to take the buckets to the cashier where she ran them through a machine. When we finished, that lady was still occupying the machine that I had dreamt about. I knew Mike didn't have the patience to wait. As we walked by, she got up.

I put forty dollars into the machine after sitting down. It only took three spins for me to get three cards for the royal flush. Looking directly at Mike, I uttered the words, "Are you ready? Here comes the royal!" Then, magically, a Royal Flush appeared before us worth $1252.34! Mike was stunned. He wasn't just stunned by what he saw, he was completely taken aback and deeply shocked.

The only things that could come out of my mouth were, "And do you remember Saint Martin? That happened also. And do you remember what I told you about the lotto numbers? Well, that happened as well. Do you believe me now?" His answer was, "Oh my God, yes!"

It was the first time in my life someone believed me. I get tears in my eyes just thinking about it. When no one believes you, it's like being accused of a crime while you are innocent. It is a horrible feeling. For twenty-nine long years, I had waited for this moment.

Although Mike was a talkative person, he surprised me by being silent and almost catatonic for three days. I was relieved that he finally knew the truth. I was also hurt that I had hurt someone again with my abilities. He truly was out of it and it broke my heart. I kept asking him, "Are you ok?"

"I'll be alright, I'll be ok," he repeated in a monotone voice.

CHAPTER 14

A Trashy Proposal

W hen an opportunity presented itself to go work for a different Poker Room, I jumped at it. The rule binder incident left a bad taste in my mouth. Frankly, it was irrational behavior, and irrational behavior scares me.

I went to work for the Gulfstream Casino. Once more, I had to witness some irregularities. As a poker dealer in South Florida, it was required to tip your supervisors ten percent of your earnings. After the poker stakes went up and were no longer a quarter and fifty cents, dealers started making a lot more money. At Gulfstream, I witnessed something new. Dealers were tipping over ten percent. And those who tipped the most got the best tables the next day. I saw dealers tip out as much as thirty percent. Human Resources wasn't even a thing yet. I had no idea what to do.

The Poker Room was relocated. It was temporarily moved to a tent near the stables. Gulfstream Racing and Casino boasted a beautiful horse track with amazing facilities. Being allergic to something in the stables caused me to have an asthma attack after spending just an hour in the tent for the first time. Luckily, this was not my first asthma attack. I knew what I was dealing with.

I was very sick during my time at Dania Jai Alai. My doctors thought it was a cold. After a few weeks of no improvement, the doctors prescribed antibiotics. As those didn't improve my situation, I was referred to an allergy specialist. The night before my appointment, my condition was so bad that I could barely breathe. When I laid down in bed, my entire childhood started flashing before my eyes. I was fearful I might be dying. Next thing I knew, I woke up still barely breathing. My appointment was in the morning. I sat in the waiting room for a very long time. Most doctors have no respect for other people's time. My lips were a light purple. When the doctor saw me, she admonished me for not telling her receptionist. I could barely talk. I wasn't telling anyone anything at that point. She weighed the options of calling an ambulance or starting the treatment immediately and ultimately suggested the latter because of her fear that I may not make it to the hospital. I knew I was going to be fine. The treatment plan included the administration of steroids and two different breathing treatments, which she promptly administered. After forty-five minutes to an hour, my lips were no longer purple. Although my breathing was still not good, it had improved. I didn't want to work in an environment that could trigger asthma attacks after experiencing them.

The next day, I reached out to Warren, my previous boss at Seminole Indian Classic Casino. "Warren, they have me dealing out in a tent. Do you have anything available?" Warren was pleased to have me back. I had the privilege of selecting my schedule. Wednesday, Saturday, and Sunday were my days off. The shift selection was mine to make, and I worked overnight since people were more generous during the late hours. Although it was the happiest point in my career, I failed to acknowledge and appreciate it.

My co-workers were fantastic. During our breaks, we would engage in friendly games of gin, backgammon, and cribbage to pass the time. Our area was hit hard by Hurricane Wilma, but thankfully, we were able to stay safe and ride out the storm in the comfort of our own homes. We often evacuated for major storms. The tropical storm was expected to arrive from the Fort Myers region, on the other side of the Florida peninsula. Luckily, our hurricane shutters were up. After Andrew, few people in Florida took hurricanes lightly.

A few months earlier, hurricane Katrina had passed through Hallandale, Florida, as a category one. No one took the storm seriously. A bunch of poker players had decided they wanted to play. They asked me to come over. When we realized the eye was coming directly for us, everyone went home. I stayed behind to clean up. When I got on the highway, I was caught in the eye. My car would hydroplane through three lanes of traffic. Right before hitting a guardrail, it would start hydroplaning the other direction, again, until almost hitting the guardrail on the other side. There is no doubt in my mind that the angels were keeping me from hitting the guard rails. That was the most scared I have ever been, yet I knew everything was going to be ok.

Katrina was a special storm. The summer we evacuated to Biloxi, my Akashic Records will reflect that while driving around, I was told by my intuition to take a good look at the beautiful homes across the street from the Beau Rivage. That they wouldn't be there forever. I had driven through the eye of the storm that my prediction had told me about. My life, so weird.

I woke up early the morning that Wilma was approaching. I could feel the change in the barometric pressure. Yes, I am that sensitive. I had nervous energy running through me. I knew I had to pay attention. It was really early, maybe four a.m. My son, who is also sensitive, got up shortly after. I could feel he felt the change in pressure as well. I was already feeling this was unusual for a tropical storm.

What happened next was beyond my wildest imagination. At around five am or maybe a little later, the rain started to come down severely. When it became daylight, I looked out of the peephole of the front door and saw what looked like nine-foot waves in the lake across the street. All the water would get pushed to one side, then the other. You could see the bottom of the lake, the floor.

This did not look like any tropical storm I ever encountered.

Throughout everything, Mike kept sleeping. It sounded like we were on and off again in a tornado. The kids were scared. Through my intuition, I knew everything would be ok. Around ten in the morning, one of the hurricane shutters peeled off from the back door, revealing the complete destruction that had taken place in our backyard. My intuition kept telling me, "You live in one of the best built houses in South Florida. The builder of Sawgrass Preserves put a lot of love into this project." I probably heard the first part at least three different times.

Though I knew everything would be fine, the already frightened children became even more terrified. That is when I went to wake Mike up.

"Excuse me, but you may want to get up now. The hurricane shutters are coming off the house."

"What? I don't believe it," was his response.

"Please come and see for yourself." Despite his reluctance, he finally put on his shorts and made his way into our dining room, where he noticed that there was a missing shutter and another one on its way out. He was stunned to see our pool was green. I told him to look out the peephole.

"This ain't no tropical storm," he said. No shit.

We were left in disbelief as we walked outside once it was over. It was as breathtaking to witness as The Grand Canyon. The destruction was so vast that it looked like a natural war zone. Our entire white picket fence was gone and almost all our trees, even most of our palm trees, were down. I think we saved two. Our pool contained pavers, furniture, and a toddler safety fence we had set up for Skye.

Our roof and all the roofs in the neighborhood were undamaged. The builder had indeed used an innovative technique or product to make our roofs so well that it made the Army Corps of Engineers do a study on some of the roofs in that neighborhood. My weirdness was right once again. They always seem to be there when you need them most.

The neighborhood was blocked. The neighbors quickly began using chainsaws to clean it up. We had no electricity. Losing power early in a storm was pretty standard for South Florida.

Flynn was Mike's cousin who lived in a neighborhood a few minutes from ours called Chateau Lane, where Mike also owned a property. That property had been lent out to friends and family, never really producing any income. Once, one of our former bosses burned down his kitchen. He stayed there for free for six months. Flynn was also our best friend. When the three of us would get together, we would just laugh the entire time. It was the most beautiful of chemistries. We used to go on bike rides that were twenty miles long. Afterwards we would play racquetball just for sport. We were both born underachieving athletes. Flynn was born with a disability that kept him from being a baseball star. I took part in every sport I could. I loved him like a brother.

Chateau Lane was less than a ten-minute drive from us. At around 1pm, Flynn showed up at our house. I was surprised he had made it there. Even though most of the roads were cleared, he informed us that a curfew at 4 or 5 pm was implemented. We took one look around at our unelectrified situation and said simultaneously, "Want to go to Orlando?"

"Kids, you are old enough to pack your own bags. Mike, go tell the neighbors where we are going and to call us when the electricity comes back on. I will pack Skye's bag."

Our stay in Orlando lasted for two weeks, with our dogs tagging along. We stayed at LaQuinta because they were pet friendly. It delighted us the next day when we went to a park and kept running into people we knew. Like us, other South Florida evacuees had migrated north to Orlando. We felt relieved after ten days when we received a call from our neighbors, notifying us that our power was restored.

Life was a mess. Mike was awaiting the outcome of his case and was not working. He kept himself busy by playing golf with Paul on most days. I couldn't blame him for his situation. I could only imagine how difficult it must have been for him to confront the charges and the potential outcomes. Because of the uncertainty of Mike's legal case, we moved to the Chateau Lane property from our beloved house. Despite being a two-bedroom townhouse, the property was quite spacious. The kids were going to share a bedroom, so we gave them the master bedroom.

We went on a cruise to Alaska. The pictures do not do justice to the breathtaking beauty of Alaska; it is truly stunning. Our experience on the Princess Cruise line ship included an incredible culinary adventure, with food that exceeded all our expectations. A diverse selection of seafood dishes awaited us every evening, with the added indulgence of souffles every night.

During the cruise, Mike and I had a great time joking about his lack of table manners. My parents were European snobs, really. Their familiarity with proper table etiquette was something they prided themselves on. I told him, "If I hit that royal flush in the casino, you have to promise to take an etiquette class."

He said, "If you hit that jackpot in there, I will gladly take whatever etiquette class you want."

I started a conversation with the casino manager. I asked him about the amount of the jackpot on the video poker machine during its last payout. He said, "I honestly don't remember."

The moment I took a seat, I started to win a little. We kept talking with the manager. The manager had just walked away when I got dealt three cards to the royal flush. I looked at Mike and said, "Are you ready? Here comes the royal." There she was, a beauty worth over $2900. Mike stood up, exclaiming, "She does it again! She does it again!" I thought he was talking about hitting the royal. No, he was impressed that I looked at him and said, "Are you ready?"

I called over the casino manager and said, "Twenty-nine hundred whatever dollars, that is the amount of the last jackpot that was hit on this bank." He looked at me, perplexed. He wasn't getting it. "I just hit the jackpot."

"Oh! Congratulations! I guess he owes you an etiquette class."

Mike never did take that class. I get so disappointed when this happens, but I also understand that it is human nature and that I'm just as flawed.

Mike's case eventually cleared up. It took over two years. It also took lots of guidance from above and a fist full of money to get him off. While his case was being resolved, we received an offer for full-time work at the Immokalee Casino property, situated to the East of the Fort Myers and Naples area, on the other side of the Florida peninsula. We accepted. Mike went there and underwent the entire hiring process. We had plans to buy a home there. Because of the housing bubble collapse, you could buy a three- or four-bedroom single family home for under 75k. After some contemplation, Flynn applied for a job at that location as well. They offered him a position. Like us, he was also planning to move there and intended to secure a home for himself.

Mike was so excited to hear that I was getting the best health insurance around by accepting the full-time position in Immokalee, that he immediately proposed to me by the garbage can in the kitchen. I had been praying so hard for seven years for this man to marry me, I never considered for a moment what was going on. He respects you so little he is proposing next to an overflowing garbage can with no ring.

Hollywood and Disney movies taught me that a happy ending is possible with love and goodness. The reality of real life is so different from those fairy tales, mankind would benefit from better examples and lessons. We would be better prepared if we were raised knowing that happy endings are unlikely in real life. Real life is a modern fairy tale, there are no happy endings. Life is more than a happy ending. I believe it is a series of lessons to help your soul develop and become more of the Light.

At a recent conference called Defeating the Demonic, the audience was so enlightened that those who could see into other dimensions were blinded by the bright light. That was just one of the phenomena that happened while we were there. How do you explain that so many people who can see into the other realms saw the same things? I even saw the same red light they did. I know they were telling the truth. Also, the lights were flickering the entire time during this event.

I couldn't believe what I was seeing. There was Mike on bended knee, next to the overflowing trash can. Believing that my love for this broken man was enough, I said yes to the garbage can proposal. He wanted to get married as soon as possible and, of course, as inexpensively as possible as well. I was in agreement, spending a lot of money on a wedding felt like taking money away from our children.

Being extremely resourceful is one of my strong suits. I had figured out that we could get married at a beautiful public park right by the intercoastal waterway for only a clean-up fee of less than a hundred dollars. There was a beautiful dock. My mother offered to buy my wedding dress. I was thrilled to find the most affordable one on the clearance rack. Happy to save my mom some money. We found rings. Hazel's best friend, a public notary, was going to be the officiant. We chose Buca Di Beppo as the reception venue. The cake was a small fondant wedding cake from a local supermarket.

I bought the dresses for the bridesmaids. My flower arrangements and bouquet were made by me. I turned to wikiHow for guidance. I was also guided to visit the Swap Shop, our town's flea market, to get fresh flowers. The Swap Shop is an extraordinary place. It had horrible energy, which of course always feels exciting. I could always feel that souls were being mistreated there, both animal and human.

They had the best and most affordable selection of fresh flowers. I bought enough for my purposes for less than two hundred dollars. Everyone thought a florist had done the flowers. The way they turned out was so impressive.

There were no clairaudient experiences on this wedding day. My intuition had been warning me for four years that this was wrong. I could feel they had given up. I really thought this was the answer to my prayers.

The grand opening of table games at Immokalee Casino was a great disappointment. They had definitely over staffed and as a result they did not hire Mike. This was a huge blow. Flynn hated his job and was more than happy to resign, counting himself grateful for not selling his home yet. I actually started praying that Flynn would find a job in his beloved field of sports memorabilia at that point. Not long afterwards, he got an awesome job in Denver, Colorado, working for a sports memorabilia auction house. He was going to be missed so much.

Mike had applied and got hired for a poker dealer job at Mardi Gras Casino, now called The Big Easy. He encountered a little trouble getting his gaming license. My intuition told Mike to threaten to sue. The day after a lawyer friend of ours sent a letter, he got his license.

Because of over-staffing, I was given the option to work only two days a week while maintaining my full-time benefits. The pay was terrible, barely reaching a hundred dollars per shift. The three-hour round-trip commute didn't make it any more pleasant. Those trips across Alligator Alley were something else.

One night, I was driving down one of the rural roads that lead to Alligator Alley after four a.m. It was pitch black. At the last moment, I saw a red, round shape. I knew instantly what it was. I ran over it in a split second. Running over this massive alligator felt like a giant speed bump. This animal was so big it took up two lanes of traffic. The one thing they teach you in Florida when this happens is you don't get out and check. I stopped for a moment, then remembered the no checking part and left. If the animal sustains an injury and feels it is in danger, it has the potential to grasp your ankles in a matter of seconds. When I lived in South Florida, stories of people being eaten by alligators were not uncommon. This was actually my second encounter with a gator. The first time I was able to swerve past it. At night, the gators are the same color as the asphalt, so they are very difficult to see. Their eyes shine red.

I also stumbled upon a lot of Florida panthers that were struck by vehicles. The species is genuinely endangered. They all have collars. I would call animal control or the relevant agency to notify them. If the panther turned out to be a female, they could save any babies. But every time I called one in, I would have to get stern with the person on the other end of the line. "I did not run it over. I'm calling so you can recover the collar and do your thing." Humans are always shocked when someone is trying to do the right thing. I'm unable to give you an exact count of the turtles I saved, occasionally directing and blocking traffic. Watch out when you pick them up. Keep them away from you to avoid being in the splash zone as sometimes they are full of water.

A week later, when I was almost ten blocks away from home, the car started smoking heavily. I took it into Mazda the next day for service. I couldn't believe my luck. "We cannot explain what happened, so our manager is fixing it under warranty. It would have been $1975, but we will take care of it."

Of course, I now understand that this is how things work when you work for The Most High.

CHAPTER 15

Someone Died Here

A fter six months of commuting to Immokalee and a lot of praying, those who were commuting from South Florida had the opportunity to meet with the table games director from the Seminole Hard Rock Casino in Hollywood, Florida. The Hard Rock was the Seminole Indians new corporate casino. I do believe because I loved the Seminoles so deeply that these blessings were bestowed on them as a result. I prayed deeply for them. It was heartbreaking to witness their hereditary congenital afflictions.

When we met with the director of The Hard Rock, the possibility of a transfer was discussed. We were informed that only part-time positions would be available to us. The combination of the daily commute and the wildlife had become too much for any of us to handle. We were happy to take any position closer to home. I knew I had to turn on the charm when the table games director started our meeting with, "You are lucky to be employed." It was quite a challenge for me because I rarely resort to insincere flattery or compliments, but I knew I had no choice. Our presence was deemed crucial by the end of the evening. We were transferred to the new location in just three weeks. God gets all the glory here. Every once in a while, when it matters, they take over my body like they did with the FBI phone call or during many traffic stops. I always know the right thing to say to get me out of a ticket. If you met me in real life, you would be highly disappointed. I'm not particularly good at anything.

When transferred to the Hard Rock, I dealt table games for a few months. Mike urged me to apply for the full-time supervisor position since it would give us health insurance again. I knew how hard full-time positions were to come by, so I applied. They promoted me. Me doing my best business was paying off and the higher ups had taken notice. Once, during a review, I performed the most incredible Spanish black-jack and regular blackjack dealing I had ever witnessed in my life. I knew I was being evaluated. I performed at a high speed. Smiling, laughing with the guests, truly a dealing machine. My supervisor could not believe I had only been dealing for a few months.

When I became a supervisor, I already knew all the rules and rulings. I went beyond that by learning how to count cards in both blackjack and baccarat. At the end of my first three months as a supervisor, they transferred me to the High Limit pit, where the least experienced super-visor had fifteen years of experience. I told the High Limit supervisors that there was a way to count cards in Baccarat. They laughed at me. My intuition had shown me this. I knew I was right. I told them that a team could come in. If they bet big at the end of a shoe, they are counting. A "shoe" is where the cards are held, but it generally refers to all the cards. They laughed at me. Six months later, a team came in. On their second night, the supervisor remembered my story and looked it up. When she brought it up to the pit boss and other superiors, she got all the glory. I didn't mind. I'm used to people not noticing my accomplishments. It made me happy that we demonstrated our knowledge to skilled players.

Mike and I had been trying to buy a home in my mom's neighbor-hood for a couple of years. Something always seemed to occur where the deal wouldn't or couldn't happen. Finally, after putting in an offer on a house six months prior, we closed on a townhouse across the street from my mom's home. The closing took longer than it ever had before. It was six months when it was usually a month or two. I failed to recognize it, but looking back I realize it was once again a sign from the Kingdom of God for me. At eighteen, I declared that my spirituality was centered on the belief that the Kingdom of God exists within me and all around me. It's my opinion that spirituality is an individual experience. Everyone's spirituality reflects their own beliefs, which is why I consider that my spirituality manifests in the way it does. If you believe in angels, then you may experience angels. If you believe in power animals, you may experience power animals. In my opinion, there is a high likelihood that both energies are essentially the same, only they are being manifested differently. I have had some contact with angels and power animals. They feel the same to me. My dream is to one day be able to talk to others like me to get to the bottom of all this stuff.

After we closed on the townhouse, I went there on my night off to clean the grout. I'm truly a night owl. I pulled my cream Kia Sorento into the driveway. As I got out, I had a clairaudient experience. A disembodied voice let me know a person died there. I rolled my eyes and thought, "Here we go with that delusion again. Even if someone had died on this property, who cares? Ghosts are not real!" I can smell bs from a mile away and the few ghost shows I had watched were bs. Up until that moment, I had never seen a ghost. I set off to clean the grout.

The next night, I finished cleaning the grout. There were no other clairaudient experiences. I am not sure if these experiences are from the Light or if they are demonic. Both of my spiritual advisors had said that if you communicate, you are probably communicating with both.

Shortly after we moved in, something inexplicable happened. We dodged a bullet by not buying a couch yet because one morning there was a lake of feces downstairs. It covered four rooms. It was about half an inch thick in the kitchen, dining room, eat-in kitchen area, and living room. Mike believed it was the dog, but the massive amount of excrement couldn't have been from the dog. It was illogical. There was almost as much excrement as there was dog. I was half expecting to find a busted pipe when I was done cleaning. It took me eight hours to clean that shit up, pun intended, all by myself.

Something very strange happened when I awoke the next day. I experienced the most excruciating headache of my life. I have some experience with migraines. My first thought was that I was having one. Luckily Sabrina, now sixteen, had her driver's permit. I told her to drive. Sabrina and Noah were living with us full time now, but Brina was still in school in Boca Raton. It was about thirty minutes north of our home. As we left Harmony Lakes, I instructed Sabrina to stop the car.

As soon as I opened the door, I began to vomit bile uncontrollably. I thought I had a brain aneurysm due to the severity of the headache. After taking out my phone, I called 911. "Please take me back to the house. The ambulance will meet us there."

They rushed me to Memorial West Hospital, fearing I had spinal meningitis due to the severe pain. Morphine wasn't working. They tried other things. I can still feel the headache today when I think about it. They did a spinal tap, everything came back normal. I informed the doctors about the bizarre incidents from the previous day. Could the mysterious feces be the cause of a parasite? The headache was awful. It went down from a ten to a nine. The pain was so severe that I couldn't control my screams every time I moved. Ten days of screaming led the doctors to consider a plasma transfusion in my spine as a possible solution.

The doctor performing this procedure was very good looking and young. Nurses were flocking around him because this was such an unusual procedure. I became worried. My intuition told me, "He's got this, all will be well." So, I stayed calm and smiled my way through the procedure. He told me, "If this works, we will know in twenty minutes. If not, we will have to figure out something else."

Back in my room, twenty minutes passed. I still had the headache. I said a prayer at this point. Asking for favors is difficult for me, even when it comes to God and the angels. A miracle occurred two hours post-procedure. The headache was gone!

The first time I had a gallstone attack was in the spring of 2011. Having never experienced this before, I had no idea what was happening. It feels like your intestines are being strangled. It was four in the morning. Mike was asleep. I knew he wouldn't drive me. I went upstairs and said, "Mike, I'm driving myself to the hospital. It seems like something bad is happening to me or I'm dying."

"Ok honey, be safe."

If your partner doesn't want to go with you to the hospital when you are in need, that may be a sign. I drove like a lady in pain. I think I was going 30 mph. The nurses immediately administered morphine. The pain magically went away. They took an MRI. I had gallstones to be treated as an outpatient. The morphine made me feel so sick that I had to call Mike to come pick me up. Now that I knew what the pain was, I dealt with the gallstone attacks on my own. I've always taken pride in my ability to handle physical pain. I just muddled through them. We went on a transatlantic cruise. On the train to Seville, I had another attack. No way was I going to a hospital. The Osso Bucco from the previous night was not a hit with my gallbladder. I battled through many of these attacks until one night. After many hours of waiting for the pain to cease, I went to the hospital. I happened to be scheduled for my last scan that day as we were going to schedule the outpatient procedure to have the gallbladder removed.

I once again drove myself and this time asked for morphine right away. I had been in this horrendous pain for hours already. The nurse seemed to agree and then disappeared for hours. After three hours in the ER, I was out of my mind with pain. I started to punch the mattress. That finally brought the nurse back. I told her again that I was in such tremendous pain, she just walked away. While she was talking to the doctor, I happened to overhear the term drug seeker being used. This prompted me to call her back in. I introduced myself as a responsible mother. I was a supervisor at the Hard Rock, where drug testing is mandatory. I made it clear that I was not a drug seeker. This finally got her to get me the morphine four hours after I arrived. After she administered the morphine she said, "Ok, you will be discharged after this."

"You are not going to take an MRI of my gallbladder?" I asked.

"No, you can just go," was her reply.

When she came back half an hour later with the discharge papers, I said, "We have a problem. The morphine didn't work. I am not going home until I know what is going on." She let out a long sigh and went to get the doctor, who finally ordered an MRI. The things I bear witness to.

The presence of a stone in the gallbladder's neck resulted in the need for emergency surgery. The medical staff sent me upstairs to a hospital room to wait for the surgery. I was assigned a room with another patient, Mrs. Jones. Mrs. Jones kept coughing and making a ruckus. At one point when the nurses came in, she told them she was dying and that she was going to die. The nurse said, "No one is dying here."

Her disruptive behavior prompted Mike to go to the nurse's station to lodge a complaint. I was surprised when they transferred Mrs. Jones to the room next to mine instead of me. Once again, I was disturbed by her noise around four a.m. from the room next door. A little while later, while a nurse was checking on her, a code blue was issued. I overheard every word. Apparently, Mrs. Jones's bed was not working. When she was vomiting, she aspirated and died because she was unable to raise herself. Everything in my body was already telling me before this happened to get out of there, but I honestly didn't have enough life experience then to follow my gut.

My surgery was scheduled for 5 p.m. the following day, which I found strange. Why did I have to wait almost 36 hours since my arrival at the hospital if this was an emergency? When I met Dr. Weinstein, I immediately said to him, "I know this is a laparoscopic procedure, but if for any reason you need to cut me open, don't be afraid to do so. I am not vain." No one ever listens to me, mostly because I am a woman. It is so annoying.

I was talking to the anesthesiologist about what happened to my former roommate that night. He said, "Yes, that was Mrs. Jones. Apparently, the doctor left some gauze or something foreign inside of her."

"And who was her doctor?"

"Dr. Weinstein." This was the last thing I heard before the anesthesia mask was placed on my face. With that, I was out. Jesus Christ himself. It was like a scene out of a movie.

I had had kidney stones before and went through procedures that required anesthesia. When you woke up, you always woke up in a recovery room. My mother underwent surgeries and also woke up in recovery rooms. I knew something was terribly wrong when I woke up in a hospital room. My intuition told me, "They are going to tell you that you are dying but you are not. We got you."

By now, I trusted my intuition a little more and that brought me great comfort. Mike was on the phone outside of my room. I heard, "No, she doesn't know yet. The doctor will be there to see her and explain things in the morning. Ok, bye mom, I love you."

"Mike!" I'm pretty sure I screamed.

"Yes?" he came in.

"First, what time is it?" was my initial question. I am almost always able to tell the time without a watch and I could not believe what I was feeling.

"It's eleven p.m." Jesus, my intuition was right!

"What is going on? The surgery was supposed to only be forty-five minutes," I said.

"Everything is fine. The doctor will be in to see you in the morning. I have to go. It's late and I have to go get Skye. I will be back tomorrow."

"What is going on? Please tell me." I pleaded.

"Everything is fine. The doctor will be in to see you in the morning." He repeated this robotically and left. I think he may have been in shock. I immediately started pounding the nurse's button.

"Good, you are up," said the nurse when she came in.

"I need to know what is going on. I know something is going on with me and no one will tell me what it is." I pleaded.

"The doctor will come and explain everything to you in the morning. I am not at liberty to say anything else," was the nurse's reply. Are you KIDDING me?

"Ok, and when is that?" I asked.

"Usually around seven a.m." I couldn't fall asleep. Judging from the communication I had with my intuition when I woke up from the anesthesia, I knew this was serious. Eight hours is a very long time to wait. I finally fell asleep at around five a.m. When I woke up, there was doctor Weinstein standing at the foot of my bed. I have a strange effect on people and many often tell me truths they would otherwise never tell.

"Good morning," he started off.

"Doctor, I'm so happy to see you. Please tell me what is going on?"

"Well, there was a lot of tinting, inflammation. I couldn't see. I cut blindly and severed your common bile duct," said the doctor.

"And what does that mean?" was my natural question.

"It means that you may have some leakage of bile into your abdominal cavity. But don't worry, this afternoon another doctor is going to put a stent in there through an endoscopy that should mitigate the problem until it's healed." I trust the process, so I thanked the doctor and waited for the other doctor to come by to tell me about the endoscopy. I did wonder, if the doctor couldn't see, why didn't he cut me open, especially after I told him to please do so if he encountered any issues? No one listens to me.

I had an endoscopy procedure in the afternoon under anesthesia. After I recovered, I was allowed to have a meal and went to sleep. The next morning, I was to undergo a nuclear medicine test to see if the stent was holding. I was taken to have this test at seven a.m. Mike, God bless him, was with me for this one. They said they had to inject a dye that would cause a funny feeling throughout my body. It was a beautiful sensation, like a warm internal blanket covering you. The test was going to take a while, an hour and a half. When the test concluded, I really needed to use the bathroom.

The intern that was there had the build of a tree trunk, similar to an athletic linebacker or a sumo wrestler. I couldn't stand up for very long, which was also worrisome. This young man said, "If it's ok with you, I am just going to pick you up and carry you to the bathroom."

When he went to pick me up, he flinched. Something had burned him. When we all looked down, there was neon orange liquid pouring out of the holes left behind by the surgery. We were all shocked. It didn't look real. The Nuclear Medicine doctor immediately started calling for a nurse. I could feel panic overcome him. They both said they had seen nothing like it before.

I still needed to go to the bathroom. That young man overcame his fear. He picked me up like I weighed twenty-five pounds and gently deposited me on the toilet. It is my belief that young man is an angel incarnated into mankind. He had zero malice in him. His energy was so light and beautiful.

CHAPTER 16

Nothing Went Right

The nurses brought a wheelchair and escorted me back to my room. The doctors informed me that the stent had failed and the fluid seeping from my body was bile. It was now a wait-and-see game to find out if my bile duct healed on its own. As a result, I was not allowed to eat or drink anything. I was on fluid IV, that was it.

There was talk of sending me down to the University of Miami because there was a specialist there that might be able to put a stitch in the bile duct. It is an extremely difficult situation to be in a hospital and not know when you are going to go home. I have been in hospitals so much now that when I go in, it truly feels like my second home. Hospitals have a strange energy. It's a mix of divine and dark energy unique to hospitals, mental institutions, prisons.

The physical effects of the bile in my abdominal cavity started showing after a couple of days. The pain was so severe I would moan in my sleep. It was like getting acid poured on your organs. I started talking to my doctors about morphine. My primary care physician was adamantly against it. Despite her warnings of addiction, she never elaborated on its symptoms or withdrawal process. After witnessing me moan in my sleep, she relented. The dosage was four milligrams of morphine every three hours. All the nurses were new. They did not know that morphine should be administered slowly to avoid the "rush". These

131

ladies jabbed that medication right in. I have to tell you that the rush feels better than an orgasm. I was smitten with the effect of the medication.

Finally, after asking Dr. Weinstein repeatedly to install drains in me, he relented. I always thought it was crazy that I told doctors what to do. My pain started improving after that. All the nurses at this hospital came from a temporary agency. You never had the same nurse twice in a row. I was a week into my initial stay when I developed a fever. The doctors started running all kinds of tests. Antibiotics were administered. Nothing was working.

One morning I woke up and I couldn't believe my eyes. My deceased father was pacing back and forth in front of my room with his hands behind his back, just like he used to do whenever I was sick as a child. I adjusted my eyes. Was I seeing things? I adjusted my eyes again. No, it was him. Then he looked up, saw me, and puff, he disappeared. I know what I saw. That was the first and only ghost I have ever seen.

My husband was warned by doctors to prepare for any possible outcome, as antibiotics had failed to treat my week-long fever. These types of blood infections often had bad outcomes. Mike was beside himself with worry. If he would have shared that with me, I could have told him I wasn't dying. He may not have believed me, anyway. Mike was so protective of me. He avoided telling me of what the doctors had informed him so that it wouldn't become a self-fulfilling prophecy. I was not concerned. Although the doctors were concerned, I had faith in a particular doctor, a deeply spiritual Jew, to find the solution. I've always had a deep connection with spiritual people and clergy. I know my case affected this man and he would find the solution.

The doctor recommended that I get up and walk around. While walking down the hallway, I collapsed and was caught by a nearby doctor as I was going down. Testing showed I had a collapsed lung from being in the same position in bed for too long. While I was down getting tested for my collapsed lung, someone stole my wallet out of my room. My intuition told me who it was, but without proof, there was nothing I could do. Everything that could go wrong was going wrong.

On the morning of my third week anniversary in the hospital, I woke up and heard telepathically, "We need you to pretend that you can't wake up when the nurse comes to check on you."

After St. Martin, I did what I was told. When the nurse came to check on me, I pretended. She went back to the nurse's station. I overheard her call the doctor. "Yes doctor, I will check her blood sugar level." I had been in NPO, with no food or drink, for three weeks. I was bed bound the entire time except for MRIs and X Rays, which were done so frequently on me that a few times we had to wait before I could legally use the machine again. Also, during those three weeks, my bed position never changed. The nurses were completely unaware that I had been laying in the same position for three weeks, which led to my collapsed lung. They came and checked my blood sugar level and found it at sixteen. That is why my intuition told me to pretend to not wake up, because my organs were under threat of shutting down.

This happened on a Sunday. Skilled EMTs from an outside team were necessary for an emergency feeding tube placement. The two young men who came in early in the afternoon could not have been more despondent. They were visibly upset to be there. When I prodded them on why, I found out it was because they were missing the football game. The fact that they were there to have the honor of saving someone's life didn't even register with these two arrogant men. I could feel every stitch that was sewn into me. Yes, a feeding tube is sewn into your neck. I hate imposing on people. These two definitely made me feel that way. I remained silent and tolerated the stitching so that they could install the feeding tube and get back to their football game as soon as possible.

The cultures revealed the type of infection I had after two weeks. It was something they had never dealt with before. My doctors were unsure of how to treat it. The Jewish infectious disease doctor had the divine idea of putting me on an AIDS medication that they usually administer in the last full-blown stages of the disease. He had no experience with this medication. I found out afterwards I was being overdosed, but maybe that was what was divinely necessary to stop the infection. However, there was a new development after I started the medication. Horrible pain in my midsection.

They sent me for additional tests several times, but they still couldn't find anything. There was good news on December 23rd. I had been fever-free for twenty-four hours. There was talk of a Christmas miracle. I might go home the next day. I was relieved that I no longer had a fever. Naturally, I wanted to be home with my children on Christmas eve. I told Mike I was going to cook Christmas dinner. On my way up the stairs, I became incapable of continuing and had no choice but to crawl on my hands and knees to reach my destination. I felt horrible. There was no way I was cooking dinner.

My mom was disappointed that I wasn't cooking. She also couldn't be bothered to come visit me in the hospital until two days before I was released. I never want to be a burden to anyone, but I was very heart-broken because I really wanted my mommy. My natural bravery has been with me since birth, but there are times when life becomes too much and a few words of comfort from my mom would have meant the world. My mother was a strange bird. She was extremely selfish in some ways and extremely selfless in other ways. When my mom saw me sit down at the dinner table that Christmas Eve, she finally understood how sick I truly was. I could feel she was finally concerned. You could tell that I had lost thirty pounds from my sunken eyes and dark bags beneath them.

I ate one bite. The children opened their gifts. Opening presents on Christmas Eve was our family's tradition. It is a tradition started by my mother, who enjoyed adult beverages with such rituals, and that was not happening in the morning. I usually also worked on Christmas Day. The casino was open twenty-four seven, three hundred and sixty-five days a year.

Afterwards, I asked Mike to call our family friend, who was also a doctor. Barry and I had one of those strong connections I talked about. We liked each other a lot. Despite not having any rights at the other hospital, he came to see me just to check on my well-being. It was such a beautiful gesture. I had only been home from the hospital for a few hours. I knew I needed help because my pain level was so intense. Barry called the hospital where he worked. He let them know we were on our way.

After a short drive, I arrived at Memorial Hospital West. The hospital staff attended to me immediately. They performed an MRI.

The radiologist came out and told me it was one of the worst cases of gastritis he had ever seen in his eight-year career. Yes, please let's get this lady some morphine and some Protonix stat. I told the nurse that I was on four milligrams at the other hospital, so that was what was ordered. Two nurses mistakenly gave me two doses of morphine within minutes of each other, which felt like a Christmas miracle. I didn't realize the second nurse was administering morphine, but I realized soon after he was done. I told him. He was talking with the other nurse and I overheard them.

"Yes, I gave her a dose about five minutes ago."

"I just gave her a dose as well."

Nothing else was said. When they came back in twenty minutes later, they found me crying. I was crying tears of joy because for the first time in three weeks I was completely pain free, if only for a little while. It is no joke to be in constant pain for so long, the last ten days being severe pain. To this day I do not understand how the other hospital didn't see the gastritis. After undergoing an endoscopy, the doctor prescribed me Protonix and a ninety-day supply of Percocet. I was sent home a couple of days later. After a week of being home and noticing how quickly my body was healing, I started vomiting uncontrollably. I became worried that it might be related to the stents that were still inside of me. Therefore, I went back to the hospital where I was initially treated and where they placed the stents. The moment they noticed the tubes hanging out of me as well as my uncontrollable vomiting, I was rushed to the back. Along with the other symptoms, I was also experiencing an intense and unbearable pain in my upper intestines. An MRI was ordered. Remember that stent they put in to bridge the hole? Well, it was now making it's way down through my digestive tract. It was a strange sensation to have an object make its rounds around your colon, and also painful. My hospitalization lasted for one more week. While I was there, I begged Dr. Weinstein to take out the drains. I had to convince him again. Once they were out, my recovery really started.

The cost of fixing me was approximately three hundred and fifty thousand dollars for the insurance company. Mike was convinced we had a malpractice lawsuit. We went to see several lawyers who all initially got very excited with my case until they found out I had health insurance. You see, in the state of Florida, Jeb Bush passed a law that prohibited anyone who survived a malpractice case to receive over five hundred thousand dollars. In Florida, any money recovered would first go to the insurance company who paid the bills. In other words, if I had no insurance, I would have been able to sue, but no lawyer wanted to take the case because there was so much money owed to the insurance.

I was out of work for ten weeks. My Table Games Supervisor job did not suit me. My department was full of colleagues who either kissed up to the boss or were ruthless. I didn't engage in such games. Prior to this, there were instances where I had been put in situations where my colleagues had backstabbed me to deflect blame from themselves. It was truly a survival of the fittest situation. Even though I saw exciting things, for me, it was not worth the hostile work environment I found myself in. I saw people buying in for amounts that were mind blowing. We had a diverse range of celebrities visit. From sports stars like LeBron James, Floyd Mayweather to folks like the cast of the Jersey Shore, who were hanging out with the Jonas Brothers. None of my coworkers recognized the Jersey Shore cast when they arrived. Despite having watched every episode, I acted like I didn't know who "The Situation" was.

In just fifteen minutes of being back on the casino floor, I was already checking my watch for my break time. I knew then I couldn't do that job anymore. Despite the celebrities and the card cheats, I was still incredibly bored. Mike was doing well at Mardi Gras. His past poker experience helped him become a shift manager. We discussed it and agreed. I again tried staying home with the kids. Skye was showing continuous signs of rebellion, refusing to go to school. Every morning, getting her to school was a struggle. Maybe with me staying at home, that would change. Ever since we moved into the townhouse where "someone died," our kid's behaviors took a drastic turn.

I gave my two-week notice the following month. My shoulder was also giving me a lot of trouble, so I thought taking more time off might be beneficial.

CHAPTER 17

This is God Speaking

Things with Skye were getting out of hand. Her dad did not allow anyone to discipline her. Disciplining her would lead to me being reprimanded and having to endure Mike's many sermons. She made sure to use this to her advantage. One morning, right after I quit my job, I was once again trying to get Skye to go to school. She was not budging. I couldn't let her win. A thirty-minute battle that involved horrible screaming ensued. After dressing her, I grabbed her by the back of her neck. I guided her down the hall, down the stairs, and into the car. I made sure she was inside before letting go. She was not hurt in any way. I wasn't applying much pressure. She argued with me the whole way. I dropped her off at school. The situation left me completely over-whelmed. I was enduring. This happened every morning except for the neck grabbing part. It was a horror show. Things only got worse with Skye. There is a television show called Evil Lives Here where children have extreme behavioral issues. That is exactly what it was like living with Skye.

That day, after I got back from dropping her off, something came over me. I did a deep cleaning of my home. I also cleaned the fridge. When I was done, everything was just so. I was really enjoying being a stay-at-home mom and having a clean house. Much to my surprise, the doorbell rang about ten minutes after I finished cleaning. It was an agent from child protective services. The school called her. Apparently, after I dropped off Skye, she went straight to a guidance counselor and told her I had punched her in the face.

I told the social worker that what they heard couldn't have occurred because we don't support physical punishment in our household, as my husband was strongly against it. She could tell by my tone I was serious. Once my interview concluded, I said to the agent, "Skye will be home in forty minutes. You are more than welcome to stay and talk to her."

"Yes, please. Also, would you mind if I inspect your home? The fridge needs to be inspected by me as well. Is that ok?"

You could eat off of the floor of my house that day. I couldn't believe that was the day I had everything done. The feeling of utter gratefulness that I felt that day should be something every human gets to experience at least once in their lifetime. I had even taken the time to make the fridge look like a store display. It was crazy. I rarely paid that much attention to detail. Though I am a perfectionist at heart, I also understand my limitations and my flaws.

Skye came home to find the investigator waiting for her, causing her to turn white as a sheet. She was taken to another room, where the evaluation process began. I could hear Skye fessing right up that she had made it all up. She said I grabbed her by the back of the neck and forced her into the car, which I had already admitted to. She asked if I physically hurt her. "No, but I don't like it when she grabs the back of my neck." The rest of the questions were routine. All went well. The investigator apologized for the inconvenience and went on her merry way.

Things with Skye were getting worse by the day. It got to the point where I couldn't take it anymore. I told Mike that I was going to cash in a favor with someone who owed me at the Hard Rock Poker Room. I was going back to work. While we had our home game, we taught a few people how to deal for free. Two of those people used to hang out with us after hours when we went out to bars. We were fond of these guys and were happy to teach them poker to help them leave the carpet cleaning profession. The two of them got jobs shortly after completing our class as supervisors at the Hard Rock. They had risen through the ranks. One had become the dealer coordinator and the other a shift manager. They were both such wonderful humans; they deserved all of that and more. Needing a job, I applied for their summer event that featured a five million dollar guaranteed prize pool, rivaling the World Series of Poker. They offered to get me in for the event, but couldn't guarantee anything afterwards because of a hiring freeze. However, they promised to try their best to keep me there.

I dealt the event. I loved dealing poker. It was and still is my absolute favorite job I ever had. I remember when I started my coworkers told me to give it six months, then I will hate it. Six months went by. I said to them that it had been six months and I still absolutely love it. "Ah, give it a couple of years." I never tired of it. I felt blessed every day I would go into work, especially after my years in table games.

My shoulder was definitely an issue. My mom was giving me a few of her oxycodone pills to help with the pain after I had finished my medication. As a sensitive, everything affects me way more than most humans. I could only tolerate a quarter of the pill without getting nauseous. It was a very slow progression. I took two quarters to get me through work for about six months. Then it became half a pill twice in one shift and maybe a couple on the weekend, as my shoulder was definitely getting worse. Multiple emergency rooms I went to would scan my shoulder and provide me with any prescription I requested. I have a genetic disorder that grows bone spurs throughout my body and one had grown around my shoulder area. It was rubbing against tendons, causing massive inflammation. Then I started taking Percocet, just as prescribed, and getting prescriptions from different doctors. My mother, the one who had taught me to never touch cocaine or heroin, was the one who encouraged me to take these medications. Like many, she was under the illusion that they were good for you because a doctor prescribed them. My mom was very intelligent. I trusted her advice.

Once the five-million-dollar tournament ended, they kept me on as a temporary hire. The director was much impressed by my dealing skills. Once again, doing my best was paying off. Dealing Poker really worked well for me. I have energy issues. Being able to sit while working and getting ample breaks was a great perk of the job. On average, you dealt a few hours, then you would receive a half-hour break. Dealing any game requires a lot of concentration if done properly. Many games require doing constant simple math problems in your head. These breaks are meant to keep you sharp.

On October 30, 2013, I giggled to myself for having the courage to go to work without makeup while also wondering why I was so tired that I hadn't applied makeup. I'm under no illusion about my appearance. I feel makeup helps me put a better face forward. It's more like a kindness for others, so they have something prettier to look at. I don't wear it because I'm vain or personally care. I rarely wear makeup at home.

For the last few weeks, I had been going around saying that God couldn't exist because of the Bible. How and why would any God allow a book that condones the stoning of women to be used as religious text? Whenever I told anyone that God wasn't real, something strange would occur. I would have the beginnings of a panic attack. I realized that my brain and soul were not in harmony. As I walked through the alley behind the Hard Rock Poker Room, an energy distortion caught my attention twenty feet above me. It was a field of consciousness without form. Thank you, Jason McLeod, for putting it into words for me. It was as if the air was bending. There was a deep booming voice that said, "This is God speaking." I immediately looked around to see if anyone else was seeing and hearing what I was, but there was no one around. I immediately thought, "This is way cool, but once again, no one is going to believe it."

Then there was a private message that concluded with, "Again, this is God speaking."

The energy that came to me at four and during Sabrina's birth was the exact same. It was definitely the energy I recognize as God, Nirvana, a warm blanket of completeness and total love. However, I have never put it past the Darkside to have tricked me in this way. My intuition always asked me to stay objective. Afterwards, the line was left open. It was like a midair phone call. Perhaps God was waiting for me to speak or ask a question. I remained quiet while smiling. I didn't want to say the wrong thing. This was actually God I was speaking to. When that line remained open, I heard different voices that sounded unenlightened asking, "Who is she?" "Why is God talking to her?"

I asked myself the same question. Did this have to do with all that

Joan of Arc business? Telepathically, the voice of the woman who helped me as a child came on. The answer was yes; it had to do with the Joan of Arc thing.

"Ok, great, why come and talk to me now?" I asked.

"Because you are about to get addicted to drugs," was her response.

"Should I not get addicted to drugs?" was my next question.

"That is up to you."

"This thing God was talking about. When is it supposed to happen?"

"About seven to ten years from now," she answered.

In order to develop more compassion for my sister's addiction, I needed to understand why addicts struggle to overcome their addictions. I was having trouble relating to their inability to quit. "I also want to tell God that it has the wrong address, that I am the poster child of sin." This was the last thing I heard.

"All of that will be explained someday."

Following this, I made a choice to prioritize my health just in case. I mean, if I'm here on a mission from God, I should stay in shape. I became very interested in the idea of learning how to run. It was something I always wanted to experience, but couldn't figure out.

A coworker changed his shift to mine shortly after I met God. He was also from Spain. He and I began our careers at competing casinos in the same year. I was hired there after auditioning, but before auditioning for the Seminoles. I found it strange that I had never heard of him before. His name was also Michael, Miguel. And when he changed shifts, of course, we hit it off. He was also a part-time soccer coach and was more than happy to teach me how to run. After a few weeks, we met at Vista View, a local park, where in a matter of a few minutes Miguel taught me how to run. The key for me was foot placement and air intake. He showed me a technique where you breathe in through your nose and mouth at the same time. I was off and running.

I couldn't believe it. This was a lifelong dream for me. I started running regularly. Miguel would join me sometimes. It was so much fun. My intuition did not like it one bit and kept telling me to stop running. I now understand that I have energy issues. I have come to a compromise about running. That said, my intuition encourages strength building exercises. It loves Pilates for me. I now run short distances often and walk in between. Not all the time, either. I now consider running a treat. It's my belief that running could also lead to knee and hip damage.

Miguel and I started training for a triathlon. When spring arrived and it was time to hit the pool, I realized my shoulder injury meant a triathlon was out of the question. Being a great swimmer, it made me really sad. I even created my own swimming stroke. Every time I would try to get in shape, I would get this really strange abdominal pain. It is very difficult to describe because it didn't quite feel of this realm. This mysterious illness caused me to be hospitalized many times. I would endure it for some time. The first time I thought maybe it was a strange presentation of a kidney stone, so I went to the emergency room of the hospital where my common bile duct was cut.

My strange abdominal pain led to many hospitalizations. Once, I was diagnosed with ulcerative colitis. When I went to get a colonoscopy three weeks later, the gastroenterologist said he couldn't remember the last time he saw a colon that was that healthy and told me I didn't need another colonoscopy for at least five years.

Another strange thing was happening at home. Every few weeks, I would feel like I was getting poked in my rectum. I dismissed the idea of it being a spirit, even though the thought crossed my mind. It hurt so bad I would immediately call on God and within thirty to forty seconds, it'd be over.

One night I woke up and I couldn't move. I was trapped in my own body. When I was a child, I had this experience and my mom dismissed it as a dream. But I wasn't dreaming. I laid there. After fifteen minutes I went into what I like to call my yogic state. I would put myself in a trance for five minutes at a time. Every five minutes, I checked if I was able to move. It was the longest two and a half hours of my life. Thoughts of my friend Petey Wheels ran across my mind. Petey had woken up one day at the tender age of eighteen to find out he was paralyzed from the waist down. Can you imagine? The most incredible part of this story is that when you met him, you didn't even realize he was in a wheelchair. He always had a funny joke or kind word ready for everyone. I think he even went skydiving. He had such joy for life; it was contagious.

During this period, my kids, who had made a commitment to never smoke, use drugs, or consume alcohol, were becoming increasingly curious about these substances. My own opioid consumption was increasing. One day at work at the Hard rock Poker Room, I was dealing the highest buy in poker game. A young man sat down at the table. One of the players recognized him.

"Hey aren't you that guy from YouTube? The guy with the opiates?"

"Yeah man, that's me."

We were all captivated by the new player's stories about his experiences with opioid addiction, which he had documented in a series of YouTube videos, complete with instructions on how to extract the drug from acetaminophen or ibuprofen. After experiencing the devastating effects of opiate addiction firsthand, he turned to making videos as a means of warning others about the dangers of these drugs. He also shares personal stories of friends who have tragically overdosed on opiates.

After all the excitement simmered down, I was able to ask him if he went to rehab to get off the meds.

"Fuck no."

"How did you do it then?" I asked.

"A fuck load of Xanax and a fuck load of weed."

I thought to myself, "Well, that leaves me out because I can't stand Xanax and I will never smoke weed." Then I had a strange clairaudient experience. A disembodied voice said to me, "You will smoke weed and lots of it." Insert eye roll.

CHAPTER 18

Faux Appendicitis

Back in 2015, Mike and I found ourselves on the verge of getting a divorce. I had seen the possibility of what a different partner would look like while hanging out with Miguel. That house had us all on edge. I was now receiving my own regular Percocet prescription from a pain management doctor. My primary care physician referred me to him because my shoulder was severely injured and I could not move my neck. I was taking the pills every six hours as prescribed.

Mike asked me to attempt to increase my dosage. I told the doctor the medicine wasn't cutting it. I used to be easily influenced by those around me. That is why I now surround myself with the highest caliber of people. I was surprised when the doctor told me that taking two pills for a boost is okay. He also said that the medicine usually wore off after four hours, not six, as the prescription directed. Ok then. The first time I took two, I couldn't believe it. It was like I just had a small shot of morphine.

Skye had stopped going to school altogether. She was placed under Baker Act, also known as the Florida Mental Health Act. It focuses on providing emergency mental health services. She was acting so out of control that we were at a loss on what to do. From my perspective, the therapist she was seeing only made things worse. There were zero resources for families in this type of situation unless you had a lot of money.

The only way I knew how to cope was through the pain meds I was taking. If taking two pills was no big deal, was three? What happened when you took four? And so, the opioid escalation process began. Eventually, your body develops a tolerance and requires more to feel the same effects. In my opinion, they are not great at taking the pain away, but they are great at making you feel like you don't care about the pain. When I was a kid, I felt complete, perhaps because I was more connected to my spirit. I'm not sure. When I tried opiates, that was the closest I had ever come at regaining that feeling. I really believed that I fixed myself.

I reached my breaking point with Mike. I was ready to divorce him, but his tears stopped me from doing so. It goes against my nature to hurt another person. I would gladly sacrifice my own happiness if that meant he was happy. The fact that I had only seen him cry twice before made it all the more moving when I saw him cry again. I promised not to leave him and committed to doing everything possible to rekindle my love for him. I was prepared to sacrifice the rest of my life to be with someone I was no longer in love with because I believed that is what God expected of me. By making such significant sacrifices, you are able to experience a feeling of contentment and selflessness as you prioritize the needs of others. You choose to put your own happiness aside in order to avoid causing harm or offending a higher power. It feels good in that way, but what a price to pay. I've come to the realization that Yahweh wants everyone to be happy, even if it means ending a marriage.

Things were so extreme at home. Skye started smoking weed. We tested Noah for drugs and he came up positive for meth. I called the cops. I was told there was nothing they could do. I asked the cops, "Don't you want to question a fifteen-year-old about where he got it?"

"No ma'am, there is nothing we can do. We can talk to him and try to scare him into not taking drugs again." I pleaded with them. There is zero help for these kids in Florida.

Mike asked me to quit my job at Hard Rock and work with him instead. He promised me he would help get me hired as a casino manager at his casino. I left the Hard Rock. Mike became a very devoted husband. He even started doing the dishes once in a while. I truly loved this man and did my absolute best to make things work with him.

In December 2015, I was offered the position of casino manager. I accepted the job. I was easily the manager with the most casino experience and that was no accident. There was a reason why inexperienced managers were hired. The things I saw at the casino could result in legal action against me if I write them in this book. Let's just say I had to go there to witness some things for God. This casino was privately owned by two cousins. A legal dispute arose between the two families after the death of one of the owners. They had trouble meeting their payroll obligations because the lawsuit resulted in their cash being frozen. The casino had to lay off some of their employees due to the circumstances and used the "last in, first out" method. I was shocked when I was laid off in February.

I was so stunned. Mike had money stashed away that he never revealed to me. He always thought I was with him because of money. One day, he looked at me in disbelief and said, "You really are not with me for the money. You really do love me." He said this several times around the time we went broke. I have never cared for money. If I ever needed money when I was younger, I would be able to play a certain poker game and win what I needed for my phone or electric bill. I understood somewhere in myself that what would happen between me and money was not of this world. To lift my spirits and maybe partly out of guilt for making me quit my beloved Hard Rock job, Mike produced that money he had squirreled away and told me to start thinking of a business I wanted to open.

One afternoon, the mysterious abdominal pains started again. I experienced pain around my appendix while Mike was at work. It dawned on me that if it was actually appendicitis, it might be a serious situation. I called Mike. I let him know that I was taking an Uber to the hospital because I wasn't fit to drive. He said he was leaving immediately. He was meeting me at the ER of the hospital I went to for the gallbladder mishap, as they were the quickest. Mike had become very attentive since our near divorce. He made me laugh every day. We always had things to talk about because he was so smart. Intellectually, we were a great match.

"I get these mysterious abdominal infections, but this one is going to present as appendicitis," is what I told the ER doctor. He looked at me bewildered and asked if I had a history of kidney stones. When I said yes, he said, "I'm pretty sure it is going to turn out to be kidney stones." Can you imagine saying to this doctor, "I am an empath who has met the Creator and my psychic abilities are telling me that this is faux appendicitis?" I would be transferred straight to the psych ward.

I played the muggle game and said, "You may very well be right." When Mike arrived, he brought me a burrito. I told him the doctor thought it was a kidney stone, not appendicitis. As I was finishing the burrito, the doctor came back with my scan results.

"I am stunned. You were right, Mrs. Litvin, it is clearly appendicitis. We have to prep you for surgery immediately." Oops, I just had Taco Bell. I was aware from past surgeries and procedures that eating before surgery was not a concern for me. Once, I had breakfast before anesthesia by accident and didn't experience any issues. I was not concerned about that, but I was concerned about having surgery in that hospital. The aftercare was so horrendous. They had their best surgeon who had operated on both my mother and my daughter come talk to me to see if he could talk me into staying. "No way, no how." I heard a patient die because of their negligence. The last time I had surgery in that hospital, the wrong organ was cut. I was not wrong for not wanting to be operated there. Plus, they weren't taking my "mysterious abdominal infection" seriously. I asked for the scan. Mike and I went to the other hospital.

After looking at the scan, they confirmed it was indeed appendicitis. I was told I needed immediate surgery. I tried to make the Eastern European surgeon understand it seemed like appendicitis, but it wasn't. That I periodically got these mysterious abdominal infections. My concerns fell on deaf ears. There was great pressure to get me to the operating room.

I woke up in the recovery room this time, which was good. The instant I woke up, I could feel all the pain from everything that had been done internally and externally to me. All I could do was mutter pain. It was not the worst I've ever felt, but probably the third worst ever. There have been so many procedures done on me I don't have enough room in this book. But I have experienced pain so severe that I have almost passed out. The nurses started administering some bs like Toradol. All I could say was, "No, seriously bad, and extreme pain." Even after the morphine, it was still very intense.

I went to sleep in a hospital room that night. Whenever I have a fever, I have the same recurring dream. It's happened since I was a child. I knew I had a fever while sleeping because of the dream I had. As soon as I woke up, I called the nurse. I told her I knew I had a fever while sleeping. She said, "Well, if you don't have a fever now, I have to send you home. We need the bed."

"The incision site looks red and angry." I pointed out.

"That is normal," she replied. "You currently have no fever. I'm getting your discharge papers."

I was in disbelief when I called Mike. My only option was to take an Uber home. I made sure to ask before I left, "How much fever do I need to have before they will admit me back?"

"39.1 Celsius."

"OK, thank you."

She rushed me out of there so quickly that I realized I still had the iv site in my arm when I was in the Uber. I had enough experience to remove it myself, fortunately. I returned home and went to bed. I knew it was only a matter of time before the fever returned. At around 8 pm, I started experiencing the initial symptoms of fever as Mike arrived home from work. Being a sensitive person, I can detect the onset of fever instantly. We started measuring the fever. At around midnight, I hit 39.1 Celsius. Mike became horrified when I got up to walk into the bathroom. What he saw was a bright red rash that covered my back legs, buttocks, as well as the small of my back. My trust in God kept me from being scared.

We returned to the hospital's emergency room, where I was left on a gurney in a waiting area for thirty-six hours since there were no available rooms. I found out that my surgeon had okayed my discharge because he was going on vacation and couldn't have any pending cases. His boss came down to take a look at me. By the next morning, the rash had spread all over my back and front. My arms and face were the only parts that were left untouched. It was unnerving to see, even for a seasoned doctor. Since I feel the emotions of others, I could feel both his genuine concern for me and disgust with the surgeon. I promised him I wouldn't sue during our heartfelt conversation, but to please do everything possible to fix me. I also told him that I tried to tell the surgeon that this was no appendicitis, that it was an abdominal infection that had now spread to the outside of my body. He agreed and promised to do everything possible to fix me.

After being taken upstairs, I had an unforgettable experience. The feeling of death was present and surrounding me. I knew I was dying. For the first time in my entire medical history, I was scared. My trust in God has kept me fearless, for I have witnessed the Creator of this Universe do the impossible. I couldn't believe what I was feeling. It was death; I was sure of it. This time my intuition was not telling me that everything would be ok. Even after five days, the antibiotics didn't work. The doctors were getting nervous. As soon as my doctors walked in, I would check how they were feeling. How they are feeling is the truth because they might try to lift your spirits up or avoid upsetting you by telling you a song and dance.

I was freaking out. Not only did the rash remain, but I also grew an abscess the size of an Easter egg at the operation site that even the doctors were amazed by. Death was still hanging around. I did the only thing one can do in such a situation. I started praying. I believe God, Yahweh, is always happy to hear from us, even if it's "just when you need a favor," Jelly Roll.

After reciting The Lord's Prayer, I received a telepathic message from my father informing me what I had to do to save myself. I doubted my sanity. I wondered if I was hallucinating, so I dismissed it and rolled my eyes, as usual. Later that day, I took a nap. In my dream my father came to me and said, "I have made a deal with God to save your life."

"God? What do you mean, God?" I asked. I have the ability to control my dreams.

"I don't have time for that." Meaning he didn't have time to have an existential discussion about God. Remember, my father was a proud and loud atheist. He told me exactly what I had been told telepathically. I had to ask the nurse to get me a ton of water and then drink until I felt nauseous or as if I was drowning. He also said to please think of a way to express gratitude for this miracle.

As soon as I woke up, I asked the nurse for three pitchers of water. I started chugging like a college student with a funnel being initiated into a fraternity. I can't remember how much time passed or if more pitchers were ordered, but I do remember getting to the point of both almost puking and feeling like I was going to drown. It was clear that I had to stop.

To the relief of the doctors, the antibiotics started working within 24 hours. The rash started receding. Death was no longer around. The doctors were so happy; it was awesome to feel their relief. I had to undergo another surgery to get rid of the abscess, which made me anxious because my experience with surgeries wasn't good. A few days later, I had that surgery. I prayed just in case before it.

I made a genuine sacrifice when I promised God to get a tattoo, something I never imagined doing. This miracle was so powerful that I made a promise to Yahweh that I would get a tattoo of a dove, which is my symbol for Him. As a child, my intuition always led me to white doves and emphasized the significance of world peace. I envisioned the tattoo in my mind's eye. A dove with a mandala on its chest. I planned to incorporate water droplets as a tribute to the life-saving properties of the water that saved me.

CHAPTER 19

I'm Sorry, Mom, She is Dead

Following the last miracle, I became more serious about my health. I started drinking more water and started paying attention to my diet. I still believed that it was ok to take these opioid medications because a doctor had prescribed them. If you asked me at that time if I was on drugs, I would have told you no and believed it.

I didn't know how to cook yet. Growing up, I always ate home-cooked meals made with fresh and wholesome ingredients. For years, Mike and I went out to dinner every night. The prepared food I was eating didn't feel the same as fresh food. The restaurant's food lacked nutrients and frequencies for me. Learning how to cook with fresh ingredients became a priority. That's the reason I visited various farmer's markets.

Most of my professional career, I had worn either a uniform or a suit. At these farmer's markets, the women were wearing these beautifully colored pants, loose fitting, looking very relaxed. You would definitely characterize it as hippie clothing. Marvelous flowy skirts, comfortable sandals. I was like, what am I doing? This is how I want to exist. I went home and told Mike I was changing my wardrobe and clothing style. He was amused.

I set out to find hippie clothing. It was very hard to come by. Apart from a high-end store in Palm Beach, we had no local stores. I let Mike know I made a decision about our business plan. "We are opening a store that sells hippie clothing." We went out and scouted locations.

In Downtown Hollywood, Florida, you can find locally owned businesses and indoor-outdoor cafes in a unique area. The atmosphere was earthy and hippie-like, and rents were cheap. We found an amazing location one street over from the main drag. It had these beautiful columns. The ceiling was vaulted in a semicircle with clouds painted on it. It was perfect. I found wholesalers for everything we needed. The vision for the design of the space was immediately clear in my mind. We bought used bakers racks and a really cool entertainment center from the Salvation Army furniture store. I repainted them all with a light gray color to match the faux stone wallpaper my sister Nicole and I installed. Nicole was down for a visit around the time I was setting up the shop. We had an absolute blast hanging up the paper. Nicole and I work so well together. I also ordered some industrial pipe store fixtures from Alabama. In the center of the store, I placed a wooden flower cart to showcase accessories. I worked around the clock. I found an amazing granite kitchen island on wheels on Craigslist for $150. If you saw this thing, you would never believe what we paid for it.

We had a handyman who was such a beautiful soul. He had an amazing skill with fabrics. We draped a beautiful mandala drapery along the base of the island, which looked both professional and rad. It definitely set the tone for the place. A beautiful decal with our logo was installed on a glass interior window behind the register. Our dressing room was both large and beautiful, featuring a bamboo chair, a full-length mirror, and various industrial pipe hooks.

Though I still have workaholic tendencies, I now strive to balance life. If I like what I am doing, I am happy working twelve to fifteen-hour days. Pricing everything turned out to be the most unexpectedly time-consuming part. I came in five thousand dollars below budget for the interior design.

This was supposed to be a family affair. The kids had all expressed excitement at the possibility of us owning a store. They had all said they would work there. And so, the Boho Story store was born. I came across a lot of ethical traders, organic clothing, and upcycled goods. I made half the store either organic, ethical, recycled, or local artisan. Local artisans had the opportunity to sell their goods for a small commission. The other half was still bohemian clothing, only it was inexpensive and fast fashion.

Our store was so dope and so well done folks would often ask me if we were a franchise. When I was buying everything for the store, I was definitely being guided. I would tell folks it was like I had angels sitting on my shoulders. I would envision something I needed or wanted for the place and suddenly I would go into some store and I would walk right up to the item I envisioned. This helped me get the store set up in record time.

Years back, as a side hustle, I used to sell costume jewelry I got on auction on eBay for between twenty-five cents and a dollar a piece. By reselling each piece for five dollars more, I could make some extra money. Some of this stuff was really nice. I had some inventory left over that didn't fit the new place's aesthetic. We printed postcards that offered a free gift to distribute around town and increase foot traffic. Once the kids had given out cards a few times, they were done. Distributing those cards required me to process a lot of strange energy, which I couldn't handle because I didn't know how to shield myself from the energy of others then. Bless Mike for coming in after work and during his off days to hand out cards. Our little gimmick worked. Most folks appreciated the gift.

We were also selling our townhouse. You know, the one where "someone died in." Our whole family was in such an awful place. Noah continued doing drugs. He had attempted to set the house on fire. My intuition showed me and I found him in the closet under the stairs, trying to set fire to the ceiling. He also had introduced Skye to marijuana. I was terrified. The words from recess as a child ran through my head. Skye smoking marijuana was a dangerous situation.

While finalizing the sale of our home, my mom frequently asked me to walk her dog, a task usually performed by my sister Hazel, who lived across the street. On a Tuesday, when I once again went there to walk Mia, their dog, my sister was laid up on the couch. When I asked what was wrong, she said that she had hurt her leg and did not want to go to the hospital. Instead, she planned on using my mom's oxycodone and Percocet to self-medicate. On my walk home, I called my sister Nicole and said, "You better get ready. It won't be long now before Hazel dies. She started taking mom's meds and her body will not be able to tolerate it." My sister was as full-blown an alcoholic as an alcoholic gets. I remember being as young as ten and watching her start her day with a beer.

Two days later, my mom called. Could I please come and walk the dog? "Of course, mom." We were still in bed, but awake. My mom was already outside walking her yorkie with a walker when Mike and I got dressed and crossed the street.

"Mom, we got this." I took the dog from her. Mike and I walked around the park with the dogs. While dropping off Mia, I found my mom sitting at the bottom of the stairs, which was an unusual spot for her.

"What is wrong, mom?" I asked.

"I have called your sister repeatedly. She needs to get up. She has a doctor's appointment at noon. Would you please go and wake her up?"

"Sure mama." I went up the stairs. As I walked towards Hazel's room, I caught a glimpse of what I thought was dirty laundry on the bathroom floor. I went straight to her room where I observed that her bed had been slept in, but there was no sign of my sister. I became apprehensive and now curious about what I had seen in the bathroom. It took me two minutes to muster up the courage for what I was about to witness. I also knew that if it was her, I wanted to be the one to find her and not my mom.

I approached the bathroom slowly. I was shocked at what I saw. My sister's body was a deep purple. She was doubled over in the bathtub, taking the shower curtain with her. I ran out of there. I broke it to my mom straight up, "I'm sorry mom, she is dead. I have to call 911 right away."

"She is dead? I want to see her body," was my mom's response.

"Absolutely not. Mike, she cannot see the body like this." Not only was she purple, but she was nude and in an obscene position. No way my mom was going to have that imprinted in her mind for the rest of her days. I called her daughter in Spain, my niece, and then my sister Nicole.

"What did I tell you two days ago? That Hazel was going to die. I'm sorry Nat, but it happened. I just found her in the bathroom."

That was when I had my first conscious thought of getting off of this stuff. I immediately started taking less and making inquiries on how to get Suboxone, a medication supposedly designed to get you off opiates. I had suffered heart palpitations that scared me. That truly was the beginning of the end for me. Everyone is different. Some people can quit cold turkey and some need time for their brains to adjust to the absence of the chemical. I belong to the latter kind. My intuition was very clear about this. In order to avoid relapsing, I had to reduce my intake every three weeks, no sooner.

After my sister's death and the sale of our house, we moved in with my mother to help with finances. I was not looking forward to this, but I always promised my mom she wouldn't have to go into a nursing home. I could feel this was part of that promise I made as a child. My mother was a control freak who had to be in control of what everyone was doing around her at all times. I describe her as a kind narcissist. Her personality was extremely complex. She was very honest, but also manipulative and controlling. Generous and kind? Yes, but also very judgmental. I try to walk a path of non-judgment because of one thing I have learned on this journey: the more I know the less I know. How is that possible, you wonder? Through enlightenment you discover that there are so many truths to this Universe and you realize that you don't even know a fraction of anything about anything, and it is best not to judge. Judgment is natural for human beings; mankind has to discern in order to survive. However, many take it to the next level. If you only believe one thing, I tell you, believe that every human being is flawed. There is no perfect being in this universe. Not even Yahweh.

Living with my mom was very hard. When I was little, she never spoke to me, she only yelled. When I would ask her why she couldn't speak to me in a normal tone, she would answer with a yell, of course. I never took it personally. I just thought that was how she was.

When I moved into her home, I inspected the medications she was taking. It was a miracle she was still alive. Lorazepam, Oxycodone 100mg, Percocet 10mg for intermittent pain, Temazepam, valium, and some other things. On a daily basis, she also consumed a Smirnoff Ice, two glasses of wine, two or three gin tonics, and a shot of brandy before bed. I thought to myself, "No way her doctor knows she drinks like this and has prescribed her all these drugs." My mother's pain management doctor was eighty years old. He had been her doctor for fifteen years. Perhaps he was easily fooled?

I told my mom I was going to her next appointment with her. Sure enough, her doctor was beyond shocked. The most shocking thing I discovered is that my mom was selling a good portion of her pills for those fifteen years. I told her it stops now or I'm moving out. She agreed. I told her that since she only takes a fraction of what is prescribed to her, we will only go get a prescription when she needs one. Even though I had quit smoking, I relapsed for a brief period and started vaping because my mom was also a chain smoker. I was eventually guided on how to quit with electronic cigarettes by gradually reducing the nicotine level. To prevent relapse while my brain adjusted to the lack of nicotine, I was guided to reduce my intake every three weeks. In the end, I was vaping zero nicotine.

I ended up going to Holland in the Netherlands on a solo trip thanks to some strange arrangements made by the Universe. My mom kept money offshore. Apparently, I needed to go get her some money. I never knew how much, but I was instructed to go receive some money that was owed to her. I chose not to cancel my trip despite the issue being resolved differently before I left. To detox, I needed a week away from everyone. My plan was to use that opportunity to get off the meds once and for all. This was now my third attempt.

What a strange voyage it was. I made a reservation for a car rental and an Airbnb in the countryside. I was going to make my first attempt at writing this book on that trip.

When I arrived at Schiphol Airport in Amsterdam, Netherlands, also known as Holland, I went straight to Hertz to get my rental car. At the counter, I realized I had lost my driver's license. Can you imagine being in a foreign country and not being able to get a vehicle to get around? Even though I was upset, I managed to stay calm and brave. I had traveled by myself dozens of times. I needed to regroup. I arrived at the town where the Airbnb was via train. Then, I took a taxi to my final destination, a charming Dutch farmhouse that offered freshly laid eggs for breakfast every day. At the airport, I bought a few packages of cookies and a sandwich from a supermarket. I immediately started to detox. Despite taking the Suboxone medication, I quickly experienced withdrawal symptoms. My intuition had already warned me that the more times I tried, the less effective the medicine would be. I was determined to make this one the one that stuck. I was guided to take one Percocet with Suboxone for 48 hours. Then reduce to half for a few more days before switching to only Suboxone.

The first couple of days were difficult. My food supply was dwindling fast, even though I wasn't very hungry. The electric energy of Europe overshadowed any other concerns I had. I felt happy and blessed to be there. Two eggs per day wouldn't be enough for the upcoming week, and the town was a long taxi ride away. This was not going to work for me. On the third day, I mentioned to Mike that I intended to take a taxi into town and find a hotel, so I could walk somewhere and get something to eat. The hotel I chose actually had a restaurant in it. While detoxing, I began my first attempt at writing this book. I wrote and wrote and wrote. It was honestly more like a purging. In the mornings, I would go have their amazing Dutch breakfast buffet, and in the evenings, I ate only on a couple of occasions because I wasn't hungry every night. One night, a couple and I hit it off and chatted until the wee hours of the morning.

After my week was up, I retraced my steps back to the airport the night before and took a hotel room nearby. I didn't want any unpleasant surprises. I wanted to make sure I got home the next day. Quitting opiates made me feel proud as the plane took off the next day. No one back home knew. They all thought I went on a vacation.

CHAPTER 20

God is My Sponsor

My mother's care and demands were my primary focus. We had some help, but it was not enough. A little over a year after opening, I had to close my store. I became my mom's full-time caretaker.

My mom believed in psychics. I was the Universe's biggest skeptic. This psychic had predicted very specific things that came to pass. The witch, as my mom called her, told my sister Nicole that she was going to marry a man in the military and that she would have two children. My sister indeed married a Blackhawk pilot and mechanic and now has two children. One which I birthed for her and a son, conceived in vitro. My sister was destined to have children. I believe something evil caused her fallopian tubes to get blocked. She is a natural caretaker, the kind of person who should have children. She is a mature soul, has multiple degrees, and loves education and family. Mature souls covet these two things the most.

I'm an old soul. I value connection, happiness, and experiences the most. According to my intuition, there are five soul types here on Earth: infant, baby, young, mature, and old. Every soul continues to incarnate until it reaches the last stage of the old soul life path. That is the one I am on.

I have never encountered an infant soul. I have encountered baby souls, young, mature, and old. Most of the world is a mix between young and mature; it varies on the geographic area. Most baby souls can be found in the equatorial regions of the world. A propensity for violence often accompanies their deep religious beliefs. Routine is essential for them. They tend to form strong opinions quickly, leading them to hate or judge easily. They love serving in the military.

Young souls thrive on success. They have an inclination towards opulence, coveting material possessions and money above all else. They will not stop until they achieve material success. Mature souls, as I mentioned, covet family and education, but are also very emotionally charged and can love deeply. Their fervent beliefs can cause them to become tunnel-visioned and neglectful of others. Nurturing and spiritual, they carry stern spiritual beliefs.

Old souls take a laid-back approach to life and are spiritually open minded. Old souls are often here to walk their own unique path and often have unique or unconventional spiritual ideas. Those with old souls dislike drama and value tranquility and serenity. They enjoy reflecting on the meaning of life.

The witch had predicted that my mom would pass when she was 82. Ina turned 82 on December 31st, 2016. Despite my skepticism, I couldn't help but believe this woman, because everything else she had told my mom had turned out to be true.

The future was something I knew I could change. I had done it before and went against my intuition and saved Mike's life as well. He was supposed to be murdered in Louisiana. I pulled my supernatural ability card and told him that, in honor of the $1252.34, he should cancel his trip to New Orleans, which he did. There were reports on the news in the subsequent days of gangs roaming the streets, and people were indeed murdered. My intuition told me to let him go, that it was in my best interest. I couldn't let him die. I didn't trust the Kingdom of God yet. That year, I paid very close attention to her. Everything was going fine. In December, I looked at my mom and said, "Mom, something doesn't sit well with me and I feel I have to take you to the ER". This was around eleven a.m. My mother started believing I was a healer when I began caring for her. She had been walking around with a swollen foot for two years. My intuition guided me to tell her to take a cinnamon supplement twice a day for two weeks. In two weeks, her foot was back to normal. I believe that spices and essential oils are like a divine apothecary.

Essential oils and intuition played a crucial role in controlling her uncontrollable Afib, an irregular heartbeat. I used to think that essential oils were a load of nonsense. A mosquito bit me outside of my shop one day. As a child, I told God if there were ever a mosquito around that really needed a meal, that it could take a bite out of me. The representative from dōTERRA had left behind some samples for our customers to try out. Our shop's inventory of dōTERRA oils was limited, but we stocked the most necessary ones. I tried every anti itch thing they sold at the pharmacy with no relief. I googled, "Is there an essential oil that will help with mosquito bites?" Google answered, "Yes, Lavender is excellent for treating mosquito bites." I went in and took a couple of drops from the sample and I couldn't believe it. Thirty seconds later, the itch was absolutely gone. I called my sister Natalie and told her. She had been using these oils for years and had nursed both animals and people back to health with them. She laughed with delight at my new discovery.

Because of my healing skills, my mother eventually agreed to appease me and agreed to go to the emergency room, but only after we had finished dinner. Dinner was always at seven.

Mom and I got to the Memorial West ER at eight p.m., three weeks before her 83rd birthday. The doctors once again couldn't believe their eyes. They couldn't believe how coherent she was. In true Ina fashion, she telling the nurses how to do their jobs. She had a white blood cell count of 22,000. That count was no doubt produced by the large hole that had perforated both her large intestine and bladder, leading fecal matter to fall into her bladder.

They had no explanation as to how this happened. The doctors didn't think it was cancer. They wanted to operate, but needed to get the infection under control first. I prayed a lot. There was talk of a colostomy bag, which meant more gross work for me. Not that I minded doing anything for my mom, but I rather not change out colostomy bags. It took a little over a week before they were ready to operate. I recited The Lord's Prayer in prayer as I walked closely beside her gurney on her way to the operating room. Sensing divine energy, I asked, "Can we go to Holland, the Netherlands, one more time when she recovers?" I really thought what I was asking for was an impossibility. The doctors couldn't believe it themselves. There was no need for a colostomy bag. They were truly surprised. What they don't know is that with God, anything is possible.

My mom turned 83 on December 31st, 2018.

My mom had to have nurses come to the house for around three months. When she finally did recover, she unfortunately started smoking again. At the time of her recovery, she faced a great deal of financial anxiety because she was dangerously close to running out of money. I promised her that she wouldn't have to worry about money, because I would always provide for her.

We later found out that my grandmother Christina's condominium in Spain was never sold, as we originally believed. Although it had been rented out all these years, my mother never received any money. When my Oma died, all four daughters were to receive equal shares. My mom said to me very clearly that she didn't care about the rent, that she just wanted the euros she had coming to her. For some reason, my mom had to go in person to get the money. God was making the trip to the Netherlands possible. She had not been back in twenty years or more. I was so excited for her! But I also knew I was undertaking a serious responsibility traveling with an 83-year-old in a wheelchair. Although this journey was from God and I had no negative feelings, I still wanted to give her my very best.

The trip we took was unforgettable. The reason we flew into Brussels, Belgium, was that we stumbled upon some incredibly cheap airfare, and since renting a car was in our plans, we decided to go for it. I made sure not to lose my driver's license this time. The car rental company at the Brussels airport wanted an obscene amount of money for a deposit. I had to call Mike and ask him to deposit more money into my account. He had to wait for the bank to open in a few hours. Meanwhile, my mother held an account at a Dutch bank in Europe. I Googled and saw they had a location in downtown Brussels. Our plan was to take a taxi and head downtown to her bank to retrieve the money.

In the afterlife, you should ask to see me schlepping my mom and all our luggage through the Brussels airport. It was a scene out of a sitcom.

The stakes were high as we only had enough cash on us for a taxi ride into Brussels, which meant we had to find a way to get more cash. It turned out that my mother's bank was only a corporate headquarters and that there were no actual bank outlets for that bank in Brussels. I was extremely worried about the situation, because if Mike failed to get the money to us we would have no choice but to ask either the Dutch or American embassy for help. My mom stayed at the bank's headquarters where there was a really nice security guard.

I 'told her I was going to find an ATM and see if the money is there. On my way to find this ATM, I stopped by a supermarket to get my mom a snack and a refreshment. She had been without food or drink since we landed hours before. When I went to pay for those items and touched my debit card, I could feel the money had been deposited. We didn't have banking through our smartphones yet. I asked the cashier to point me to the nearest ATM, where I got a printout of my statement. The money was there. I immediately thanked God and was so grateful that we had enough money to make such a deposit on a whim.

I went back to get my mom. It was like being a contestant on my favorite show, the Amazing Race. I had gotten enough money out for incidentals and the cab ride back to the airport. My mom was so happy to receive her juice and snack. She was also relieved that the money was there. I once again lugged all the bags and her around the airport. It truly was a scene to be seen. My mother, who wasn't a minimalist packer, took full advantage of the two luggage per person policy, a personal item, and several purses. Hearing her opinion on purses was always entertaining because she firmly believed they were not personal items and would argue this point without hesitation.

The scene was chaotic, with bags on the verge of toppling over. At one point, I was on a hill. A good Samaritan helped me, thank God. Good thing I'm not easily embarrassed. My mom always had a lit cigarette whenever we were outside, which unfortunately meant I had to tolerate the smoke in my face. I endured it happily because all our troubles were paying off. The car we had reserved was rented, so we received an upgrade to a larger SUV, which the agent said was probably more suitable considering the wheelchair and the pile of luggage.

Things were looking up. I found the design of this oversized Citroen

SUV to be beautifully humbling. It also drove like a dream. If I lived in Europe, that absolutely would have been my car. The trunk was huge and all the luggage and wheelchair fit perfectly, as if it was designed for them.

The motel we stayed at upgraded us to a "family room" for the whole week. That is how it works when you are in God's army. They pay you through these types of kindnesses. Most hotels in Holland have "family rooms." The rooms are designed for families and typically have two bedrooms for added privacy. I couldn't have been more relieved. Sharing a space without walls for a week with my mom would have been a real sacrifice for me. They also had a very adequate restaurant

We spent the week traveling to see my aunt, her best friend, and her hometown. Our main reason we were there was to retrieve this money. We visited several branches of my mother's bank until we could finally arrange to receive the money. It would be ready for us at the Schiphol Airport branch a few days before our departure.

The reason my mom had this bank was because she was good friends with the former head of the bank and his wife. When we lived in Spain, they came and stayed with us multiple times. We felt like Bonnie and Clyde leaving that bank with that money. I can't remember how much it was, but it was less than we had expected. We didn't care; we were on such a high from our adventure. The next day, we returned to Brussels and went back home to Davie, Florida, where I continued to take care of her. When she started smoking again, I sensed her time was near. As I expected, she was diagnosed with lung cancer during the summer. Without my knowledge, she told the doctors that she didn't want chemo and was prepared to go.

My recovery was progressing very well. I had a new Suboxone doctor. Suboxone had taken me as far as it could. Following my intuition, I was guided to gradually reduce my dose by cutting the pills by around 25% every three weeks. However, when I reached a quarter pill, the Suboxone would crumble into dust, making it impossible to continue tapering down the drug intake. I would still go into withdrawal if I didn't take Suboxone.

I believe I am here to witness things for the Creator of this Universe. My recovery experience was part of that. When Yahweh realized I couldn't go any smaller and was still going into withdrawal, a new drug was created, called Zubsolv. This drug indeed allowed you to taper down even further. My doctor's lack of experience with the drug led to a high dose on my first use, resulting in me getting high. I was so upset because I had been clean for so long. I demanded the Suboxone back. Realizing there was no way out after a few more months on Suboxone, I went back and opted to try Zubsolv again, but at a much lower dose. My doctor agreed. This was the right path. I did not get stoned, nor did I have withdrawal. Zubsolv came in all kinds of doses that truly allowed you to taper down.

As a sensitive, everything affects you more and withdrawal for me was a death sentence. I had already tried to quit cold turkey twice, and the second time was when I discovered marijuana. The pain I was experiencing was so severe that I told God very seriously that I was going to jump off the highest point of the roof. I absolutely could not tolerate it, and it had been going on for hours. I was going to kill myself. I absolutely meant it. Withdrawal from opiates or heroin is like having every illness known to mankind all at once and that withdrawal goes on for days to where you can't hang on anymore. You have nausea, vomiting, headache, diarrhea, horrible calf and back pain, post-nasal drip, sometimes fever, inability to regulate your body temperature, and the mother of them all, panic attacks. That is why so many people relapse. No doctor ever told me about these side effects. Many doctors prescribed these medications to me. Not a single one ever mentioned any of this. If they had, I know I wouldn't have taken the medicine. For the same reason, I have never tried cocaine or anything else like that. These were doctors telling you it was ok.

Each time I visited my recovery doctor, he never forgot to ask me about my sponsor. My answer was always God. My doctor was a true believer and an old soul. He always accepted my answer, he never questioned it. Once we had a hurricane coming straight for South Florida as I was in the middle of a metaphysical battle. The information I received was that the hurricane was going to be shifted by Jesus, as my case needed no more complications. The doctor was experiencing panic because he had not boarded up his practice. I told him not to worry that the hurricane was not coming, that I had psychic ability. After the storm, the meteorologists were stumped. It had, without explanation, turned and went to the Bahamas. There were reports on the national news of people saying that Jesus turned the storm around. I felt like I was in the Twilight Zone because this was around the same time an entity that identified itself as Jesus had introduced himself to me.

CHAPTER 21

Empath

I assumed the role of my mother's caregiver in her final days, however it became apparent to me I needed extra help. Early on, we had a helper from Colombia named Idalia. Idalia had a family in Boca Raton. She would come help us during the week. Idalia and I share an unexplainable connection that I believe has existed in multiple lifetimes. She is the most amazing soul I have ever encountered and I pray loudly that we may one day be reunited again. Idalia and I would finish each other's sentences. Throughout our entire time working together, we never had a single disagreement or argument, and we always worked together seamlessly. Whenever we were together, we constantly laughed and clowned around, making every moment enjoyable. I am very childlike in the right company, as many enlightened folks are. We just came here to have a good time. Without her, enduring what I was going through would not have been possible. When I agreed to care for my mother at home as she died, I didn't realize the full extent of what it would entail. The things I experienced and witnessed were beyond the limits of what any human should have to endure. Even though I had been through a lot, I saw it as a chance to learn and an honor to be a part of. Being able to fulfill my childhood promise to her instead of a stranger was truly an honor for me. I felt privileged to do those things for her.

There had been other periods in her life when she had needed to wear diapers. Despite being in the hospital setting, she remained firm in her insistence that only I was permitted to change them, and declined any offers of assistance from others. Although it was sometimes inconvenient, I always made time to stop in before and after work to change her because of how much I loved her.

The feeling of terror that my mom had about dying was something that I could sense very strongly. "Mom, I have met God." I told her I had met The Creator, God, in 2013 while walking into work. She absolutely believed me. I could feel relief wash over her. There was no doubt in my mother's mind that I was telling the truth and not lying. I told her about my communication with my dad after his passing. I shared with her my belief in the afterlife and that I felt my dad would come to her when she was ready to pass on.

The next day, I said to my mom, "Mama, there is a good chance that Skye is going to join you in Heaven. If that happens, promise you will look after her."

"Of course, Stinje." Stinje is my nickname in Dutch. When I was little, my mother had a Dutch friend that went on extended vacations to Spain. On two different occasions when they arrived at our house, she said, "Ina, you will not believe this, but I just had Jesus in my car." My mom did not know what to make of this.

"What was he doing?"

"Sitting in the back seat," she said. The next time she came over, she had her daughter with her and they both claimed to have seen Jesus in the back seat of the car. My mother did not believe them. I could feel they were telling the truth. I felt a huge sense of relief when my mom chose to believe me after I told her I had met The Creator.

Those were exhausting days. Because of her prolonged bed rest, she developed bed sores that needed constant care. Real nurses would come by every so often, a few times a week. She was doing hospice at home. Whenever she was ready to pass away, a nurse would arrive and remain by her side until the end. On October nineteenth, a Friday, there was a definite change in her and I called the nurses. I was afraid to leave her side. The nurses couldn't come until the next day. I didn't sleep at all that night because I stayed up with her. My intention was to make sure she was comfortable. When the nurse finally arrived the next afternoon,

I think I slept like twelve hours. Idalia was not with us on the weekends, just Monday through Thursday. It took my mom four days to pass, or "turn" as the nurses referred to it. At twelve a.m. on the twenty-third, I told the nurse that I wished to witness my mother's final breath. I asked her to let me know if it was near. At around 5 a.m., I got a phone call in the upstairs bedroom informing me she was almost gone. I ran downstairs and indeed saw her take one last breath.

I didn't cry. There were things to do. It was my responsibility to call the funeral home for her prearranged services and sensed that she wanted me to change her nightgown. I put on the prettiest one I could find. After the funeral home picked up her body, I felt so emotionally drained that I went straight back to bed. I think the six months of round-the-clock care genuinely overwhelmed me. That afternoon, it hit me. Losing my mother caused me such intense pain. I hope to never experience it again. I could never imagine that losing your mom could produce such an emotion. I immediately started praying and asked God to take it away, and it was gone.

That was a pain I could not have handled.

About ten days after my mother's passing, the ceiling in the living room of that house collapsed. My mother-in-law was living in assisted living and her home had been sitting empty. The townhouse belonged to both Mike and his mother, as their names were both on the deed. According to Mike, he had paid for the home. It was already determined that we would go there after my mom's passing. The ceiling just put more pep in our step.

My mother-in-law's house needed serious remodeling. The presence of carpet and wallpaper everywhere made it unlivable for us. It was stuck in 1980. The home had a seventies vibe to it, which inspired me to remodel it in a mid-century modern style. It suited the architecture of the building. We had a Star Trek symbol made of contrasting tile put on the living room floor. I prayed for the right artisan to come to me. The whole remodel took less than two months and by January 2019 I moved us in. The place was absolutely beautiful.

I'm a Trekkie, through and through. When I have a bad day, an episode of any Star Trek series will cheer me right up. I have also met many Star Trek actors. It's like they are part of my soul family. Just

171

before the COVID shutdown in 2020, Mike and I scheduled a "divorce" cruise that was a Star Trek cruise. It was not our first Star Trek Cruise. On each Star Trek Cruise, I would overhear many say how cool it would be if Jerry Ryan, Seven of Nine, would join a cruise. One day, I was swimming at my mom's community pool and I prayed that Seven of Nine would join the cruise. At five p.m. that same day, there was an announcement. Jerry Ryan was going to be on the cruise! After we boarded the ship, we were on our way to have lunch. She was standing there all by herself by the elevators. She was literally the first person I saw on that ship. I couldn't tell her my story. My entire life, I have refrained from sharing my truths because of the people who doubted me. Meeting others like me recently gave me the courage to write this book.

I had become a regular marijuana user. I had my medical card. During the worst withdrawal I ever experienced, I tried smoking weed for the first time. I only took one or two puffs from a joint. After a few minutes of feeling no effect, I went back to bed to contemplate my options on what to do about the severe physical pain I was experiencing. I said to Mike, "I don't think this marijuana stuff works."

"Yeah, probably not," he replied.

"Do you feel that?" I asked.

"Feel what?"

"I feel like there is a motor under my butt."

"I don't feel anything," he replied.

I stayed quiet. Maybe the marijuana was having some effect. In response to the situation, I muttered, "Seriously?"" under my breath. "People do this stuff for fun?" Mike started cracking up. In a state of disbelief, I kept repeating this over and over again.

"I guess the marijuana is working". When I looked up, I was looking out of the window of a spaceship. Our bedroom had turned into a spaceship. I said to Mike, "We are on a spaceship." He was laughing with delight. I tried to get up. I knew this was not rational. As soon as I stood up, three faces appeared before me and I instantly sensed that they were my spirit guides. With just their outline visible, they were shouting at me that I couldn't use both opiates and marijuana together. It seemed to me that I was hallucinating. I walked into the bathroom. I could see the three faces. Then I heard a voice that I recognized as The Creator telling my guides to please not worry, that He would fix it. Yahweh, God, to me has no sex. I use Him because that is what is most common today, but Yahweh really doesn't have any pronouns. In my opinion, it is greater than that.

I got in the shower to see if it would lessen the impact of the marijuana. Under the water, I kept going from this reality to the spaceship. I remember looking out a porthole and feeling we were traveling thousands of miles per hour, maybe faster. I remember looking out at the space going by. The sight was beautiful and, at such speeds, space was quite crowded. We arrived at a space station, where I stepped out and was welcomed with admiration and honor by everyone who saw me. I went in and realized that my job was to feel how everyone was feeling. To make sure everyone was getting along. There was a type of promenade where commerce was happening. What I saw put Star Trek to shame. The diverse aliens, the colors, what they were wearing were beyond anything any Star Trek movie has put forth. What I found most shocking was the love and respect all these beings had for each other. I could feel it. I understood my job was to go from space station to space station as some kind of wellness ambassador. I pretty much do the same thing as I drive around Earth. If I sense negative energy, I ask for help from a higher power.

After sometime the effects were settling down, I was filled with divine energy that led to some divine love making. I understood what my guides were trying to tell me. I was already trying to get rid of the opiates. After I stopped taking the actual oxycodone type products, I did start smoking marijuana because I was guided to. I would have some very serious things that were going to happen in my life and I believe they wanted me to be in a better mental place than I was. I believe it was always intended as a path to sobriety for me.

Skye had become belligerent, and there was nothing anyone could do. Police had told us not to call anymore, and it got even scarier. My new job was to stay home with her. I spoke to Skye last night in spirit and she would like me to tell you more about her. Skye was great at everything she did, drawing, writing, acting, makeup, hair. She was so gifted. I told her all the time. She could not see that in herself. She was also physically beautiful. Her hair was a stunning shade of orange-red and her skin was as beautiful as porcelain. Her eyes were large and green. My favorite human being on Earth. I can't say anymore because it is too painful.

Her behavior was out of control when we lived with my mom, but when we moved, it escalated to a whole other level. I had had a recurring dream that Skye was going to stab me to death while I was sleeping. A lock was installed on the master bedroom door. I think we were there for three weeks when she broke the lock and made it unusable. Mike was the opposite of handy. I didn't know it at the time, but I am now perfectly capable of installing a lock. I had no self-esteem at that point.

Things with Mike had gone back to where they had been before our near divorce. Skye was not going to school. She was home all day long, verbally attacking me for hours. I did not know what was wrong with my child. When Skye was good, she was my favorite person in the whole wide world. She was naturally kind to the elderly and children. Mike had developed a new habit of going to the Seminole Classic Casino after work. He was financially responsible; I wasn't concerned about that. Skye and I were home alone for around twelve hours most days. This went on for many months. Mike still didn't believe in disciplining his child. Every time I tried it was World War three between the three of us. He never had my back. I felt strongly that Skye needed to lose all her electronics and, over the years, pleaded with him for this, but got nowhere. I believe children should have a healthy fear of their parents because if there is ever a time where their lives are at stake they need to listen.

Although I paid attention to most of my parent's teachings, I wished they had been wiser and didn't encourage drinking and smoking, especially my mom. If you came over to my parent's house, you were immediately offered an alcoholic beverage. If you turned it down, my mother would literally give you the stink eye. "Oh, you don't drink? Why not?" If you were thin-skinned, her disdainful questioning could leave you feeling small. Many would cave at this point and say, "Why not? I'll take a beer," or whatever their drink of choice was, much to my mom's delight. She was a world class manipulator.

One day I was in my bedroom at the remodeled house when Skye came in with our largest butcher knife. I remember my three

Chihuahuas getting up and standing in a formation around me, one on each side and one by my feet. I felt like, "uh oh, here we go." To my surprise, she raised the knife to her own neck. When she started cutting her own neck in front of me, I stayed calm and serene. All three of my dogs were growling at the same time. Trusting my instinct, I looked directly at her. "Skye, if you are that unhappy, I want you to go to the Other Side, so keep cutting and I will see you in the next one." In that instant, she stopped cutting, and she put her head down and walked out. There was always this smell around her, and it was strong that day. Until then, I was unaware that demonic oppression or possession were real. I had no idea what I was dealing with. Something in that haunted house we lived in had affected her.

Of course, I told Mike, but he dismissed it. I was in bed for six weeks after that incident. I was afraid to go to the bathroom. The sense of being watched overwhelmed me. I made a promise to my mom, who believed in mediums, that I would one day communicate with a medium to talk to her from the Other Side. When I promised this, I never imagined this was really possible but intended to keep my word, regardless.

We went away to Orlando for the weekend. We switched things up that year by getting Disney year passes, a big change from our usual visits to SeaWorld and Universal Studios for the past ten years. Despite being more expensive, Disney feels like a second home to me since I visited it frequently as a child and young adult. There is definitely something energetic going on at the Disney Parks, in my opinion.

Mike and my dog, Mr. Spock, were with me at a condo that also served as a hotel. While we were at the park having fun, I left the TV on a random channel for Mr. Spock in the bedroom. The TV was on a paranormal show when we returned. I attempted to watch a few ghost shows before, but as someone who can detect deception, I found them to be full of staged trickery. So, I quickly lost interest. Since we never watched TV at that time of day, it remained on as background noise. I was playing a video game when the star of the show, Amy Allen, hit the screen. At that moment, I felt the butterflies in my stomach. I knew that I needed to concentrate and give the TV my full attention.

Over the years, I had experienced many weird things. I realized that her odd abilities were connected to mine. The thought of not being alone crossed my mind for the first time. This show, though scripted, was sincere. When we got home, I watched every episode to see if at any point she mentioned God. I believed there was a link between our skills and Yahweh. God was finally referenced in one episode of season three.

I scheduled an appointment with a medium. While searching on Google, I was instantly attracted to a local medium. He was someone I was definitely meant to meet. When I called to schedule, he was fully booked for the next three weeks. I was happy. I was keeping the promise to my mom. In three weeks time I had an appointment.

I continued watching The Dead Files and continued being bed bound, but was starting to understand what was happening with me as I was getting an education in metaphysics by watching every episode The Dead Files had put out to date.

Exactly one week before my appointment with the medium, I was walking back to my bed from the bathroom when I had a clairaudient experience. "Empath." One word. On The Dead Files, they used the term, but I didn't know what it meant. I asked, "Empath?" Telepathically I heard, "Google it." I was stunned. They knew about Google? I Googled "empath." The realization that I was not alone, and that there was a term for me, left me stunned. Discovering that my perceived flaws were actually a byproduct of my empathic nature left me in disbelief. I immediately was guided to take an empath test. I scored twenty out of twenty.

I climbed onto my bed and recited the Lord's Prayer. Another prayer that came to me instinctively, granting The Creator authority over my body, speech, life decisions, and more. Everything was coming out beautifully and effortlessly, as if I knew it by heart. I asked God, Yahweh, to teach me everything I had to know about spirituality in that moment. Books, websites, and a spiritual guru were sent to me.

I made a pledge to travel in truth and honesty, which I have kept and has been a delightful part of my journey. I let The Creator know I couldn't feel any love for Him at that moment. My promise to honesty kept things very real between God and I. Today God, Yahweh, is the love of my life. Since my spiritual awakening, I have endured so many other things. Divorce after an eighteen-year relationship, I gave up all my earthly possessions to prove to the universe that I didn't care about money. I lost my best friend, Mr. Spock, and Skye is indeed in Heaven. As I write this, there's not a single penny to my name. I live through the Kingdom of God and the blessings that Kingdom bestows on me. You can count on one hand the things I own if you make an exception for clothing. Most of my wardrobe comes from the thrift store. Upcycling clothes is one of the best things you can do for the environment. That has nothing to do with money.

Years earlier, I had read the book Eat, Pray, Love by Elizabeth Gilbert. When I had my hippie boutique, women would ask me on a regular basis if I had read the book. When I answered no, I couldn't shut these women up about the book. This was before my vow of honesty. To prevent them from talking endlessly and to avoid spoilers, I pretended to have read it and eventually read the book because of these women's apparent love for this work of art. Gilbert is now my favorite author, and I have read most of her books. Consider reading Big Magic if you enjoyed my book. She is not wrong. The concept of the book is that we all share ideas. I call it a Quantum Field. It's how I'm able to read people's minds sometimes. I access their quantum field somehow, because my soul, Higher Self, is badass. The human version of me is a putz. I truly am nothing special. I don't excel at anything other than doing my best.

In Eat, Pray, Love, I came across beliefs that resonated with my own in Siddha yoga. The book had been out for a long time and I wondered if Siddha Yoga had made its way to South Florida. A Google search revealed that indeed it had. They had a temple in Miami. I asked Mike to come with me to our first visit. He agreed.

When I arrived, they were gathered at satsang, a coming together that included a vegetarian meal. I didn't say a word. One woman stood up and said, I kid you not, "She is the one." Then another stood up and said, "My God, she is the one. This one has been a Yogi before." Then a third stood up and said, "Guys what you are looking at here is the real deal. A real bona fide psychic." Mike and I just looked at each other. I walked over and hugged each of the ladies who had stood up and started telling them my stories about the lottery numbers, dreams that became reality, resurrecting the insects, and more. They do a group meditation, during which I connected with their guru in spirit. I felt he was low frequency, and I knew at that moment that Siddha Yoga was not for me. I was still very grateful for the experience.

The medium I was going to see was my first paranormal investigation. Little did I know, God had sent me on my first mission. I was grateful to have Him by my side. The medium I was going to see was possessed, just like in the movie The Exorcist. When I walked into his office, my body was overtaken and I was no longer in control.

"I'm here to witness things for God," I said.

"Ok," he said. This allowed us to proceed without violating his free will. This man, like me, knew who he was the reincarnation of. He had been around during Yeshua's time, like me.

CHAPTER 22

Greatest Minds

After my encounter with this medium, I asked Yahweh for a
spiritual guru. I quickly felt I was in over my head.

An email alert confirmed the vision I had of the Siddha Yoga temple.
I had never received any emails or email alerts from them. That was
confirmation for me. I had a vision of my guru being the first lady who
stood up and said that I was the one. Back to the Siddha Yoga temple I
went. As soon as I walked in, my guru saw me, stood up, and hugged me
tightly. I told her about my spiritual awakening and what was going on
with the medium. The medium was one with Jesus. I remembered her
telling me she had met Yeshua and Mother Mary. Of course, I didn't
believe her then, but I certainly do now!

She knew exactly what to do. She said we had to do a supplication of
an exorcism. Basically, we had to ask God and the angels for an exorcism.
She said it could take weeks and we should pray multiple times a day.
She also told me how her abilities work, about her spiritual awakening
ten or fifteen years earlier. She, too, knew who she was the reincarnation
of. The spirit of Jesus's grandmother and Nefertiti lived on in her. She
taught me a lot about how it all works. My abilities include picking up
the abilities of others. While we were working together, I could see what
she was seeing. We did healings together.

A couple of days before I discovered I may be the reincarnation of

Judas, an entity came to me telepathically and identified Himself as Jesus, Yeshua. I rolled my eyes, but He stayed with me for three days. On the second day, He came to my Zumba class with me. I had deep love and fondness for my Zumba instructor. She always concluded her class by talking about how we are one, love and light. Knowing her teaching schedule, her being overweight was perplexing. I was guided to walk up to her after class and tell her who I was the reincarnation of. I told her that Jesus and I would like to perform a miracle for her and I asked what she wanted. She said she had a medical condition that kept her from losing weight no matter how much effort she put in at the gym. I said "Done, it will be taken care of." She looked at me in disbelief. Guess who looked like a total Instagram gym rat two months later?

The next day, I was shown I was the reincarnation of Judas. I was heartbroken. Me, the reincarnation of Yeshua's murderer. I heard, "Call your guru." So I did.

"Cristina, you are not going to believe this, but I have Jesus here with me!" She was so excited. "He says he has some messages for you. You did not kill him. It was all part of a plan. Promise you will not dwell on this. He loves you very much. Again, promise to not worry about this."

I promised and for once in my life, I kept my word. Jesus was by my side, but our communication was hindered because I hadn't grasped the process. That is why I needed my guru. However, we communicated enough for Jesus to show me how to make a delicious pasta casserole. It was such a beautiful experience cooking with Him. I later on discovered that Judas took the blame to prevent a world war and that Jesus and Judas were best friends.

I followed my intuition and scheduled additional sessions with the medium. After our second meeting, when we embraced, we were both shot through the heart by an arrow. It was such a strange experience. I read one of his books and kept having clairaudient experiences that told me he was my one. I was extremely confused because I did not find this man attractive and I found him to be unqualified to be "my one." In retrospect, I now realize that his demons had jumped me.

During our last session, it was like I was in a horror movie. And guess what? I stayed calm, cool, and collected. To be honest, I sensed the presence of angels all around me. I knew I had nothing to worry about. There were two different voices coming out of this man's mouth. His and a demonic one. I can't even remember what we talked about, because it didn't matter. I knew to disregard anything this person was saying.

He had been practicing black magic. Black magic should never be practiced by anyone. He was also dating a black magic priestess who would put spells on him. It took weeks to get him free, but we did. He is the most gifted psychic in the world, per my intuition. Even being the most gifted, he scores between ninety-one and ninety-two percent accuracy. People who receive readings take that information to heart. That roughly ten percent can be the difference between someone making the right or wrong decision. I, personally, don't want to be responsible for that. I don't do readings anymore. If I ever considered doing a reading, it would be in a team. My intuition says psychics should work in teams.

After my awakening, I was informed that it was perfectly fine for me to live a regular life, if that was what I wanted. In my soul, I always knew I was meant to be a soldier in God's army. There was no choice for me. Following my spiritual awakening, I experienced what's known as the dark night of the soul. For two or three days, it felt like I was falling down a rabbit hole. The feeling of falling for hours and days on end was horrifying. My intuition very strongly advised me on what to do. Take a valium. I hated taking anything after I got off the opiates, but I listened and it was over. The dark night of the soul is such a bizarre and uncomfortable feeling. I feel it is done to motivate you to stay in the Light. To do what is right at every opportunity given to you in life.

Remember those recurring dreams I had where Skye would stab me to death? It was around this time that I was told it was time to go or that would become a reality. I still didn't listen very well. I had made a promise to Mike to stay with him for the rest of our lives, and I meant it.

Around this time, I had an unusual experience. It felt like something in my brain was being worked on for two nights in a row. The second night, I started levitating in my bed with intention. My brain was making it happen. I was hovering slightly above the mattress, attempting to get Mike's attention without breaking my concentration and losing my ability to levitate. I knew if I said his name, it was likely over. Despite my attempts to wake him up with sounds, he stayed asleep. The moment I uttered his name, I collapsed back onto the mattress.

About five months later on a Sunday, I had a clairaudient experience that said, "Your husband is not where he is supposed to be." I rolled my eyes. The next Sunday, again, "Your husband is not where he is supposed to be." Finally, on the third Sunday after I was told the same thing, I said, "Fine, I am going to go check. If he is at work, I will never trust you again." It was a forty-minute drive to Mike's work, not something I really wanted to do.

When I arrived, his car was not there. I was not a pesky wife and I'm uber independent. I was never a wife that called her husband over and over. Because of this, we had a rule. If I called twice in a row, it was an emergency and you better pick up. I called the first time, there was no answer. I called again.

"Hi honey," he said as he picked up.

"Where are you?" I asked in a monotone voice as to not give away my panic.

"I'm at work," was his response.

"No, you are not." In that precise moment, I knew it was over between us. There was no way I was spending the rest of my life wondering if my husband was where he said he was going to be. He started with all kinds of excuses that I quickly debunked and said, "Listen, I don't care where you are or with whom you are. This is obviously the end for us and tomorrow I need you to come with me to buy a small travel trailer. I am leaving."

I realized that I would need a truck since my GMC Terrain had a turbocharged engine that was unable to tow even a small travel trailer. Panic washed over me. I was at a loss on how to get a truck. I had not worked in years and was absolutely unaware of my credit score. My intuition told me to check. I couldn't believe my eyes, 720. My credit score was consistently low except for a mysterious spike to 700s when I had to purchase a house. I could feel this was God's work. Without that credit score, I would not have been bold enough to walk into a car dealership and ask to be financed without a job.

I found a brand-new trailer left behind from the previous year and got a really nice discount. It was a Forest River Wildwood FX Platinum edition. She was perfect. I named her Gladys. I walked into the used car dealership and found a Nissan Terrain pickup truck. They financed me without issues. On Friday, we picked up the trailer. While buying everything I needed for my new house, I was guided to buy bandanas to cover my face. I thought to myself, "Why would I need a bandana to cover my face? Am I going to encounter a dust storm in Texas?" It was January 2020.

In March, I drove down to Mike's home for the Star Trek cruise. We were adamant about having a cordial relationship after our separation. On this trip, I saw Skye for the final time. She was sixteen. We had one conversation. It started with her screaming at me that she didn't want to live anymore. I started explaining metaphysics once again to her. Begging her not to take my word for it, to do her own research. To please watch The Dead Files. Again, I told her I had met The Creator. She mocked me. Her father, knowing full well I had supernatural abilities, never once confirmed this to her. She didn't believe me, no doubt because he always doubted me.

She continued screaming that she didn't want to live anymore. At that moment, something supernatural took over my speech and I couldn't believe what was coming out of my mouth. "Skye, you are going to get a couple of stints in rehab. It is your choice. You don't have to live like this. Addictions creates an agreement with the Darkside, allowing it to influence your mind and feelings. The angels will protect you until you are eighteen. If you still don't want to live then, don't be surprised if you die." I had goosebumps and shivers all over me.

With Jerry Ryan coming onboard, I knew this was going to be a special voyage. COVID was a thing already, but in the U.S. it was still business as usual. I immediately had the boat blessed and protected against COVID . The last time I checked, The Explorer of the Seas, was one of only two ships that never tested positive for COVID . I reassured the other passengers that there was nothing to worry about as I had met The Creator and the boat was protected. Every single time I got an eye roll. I didn't care. I knew I was planting a seed for posterity. When I said my protection prayer, I heard, "We are in agreement. Some of the greatest minds of mankind will be there. The ship will be protected."

Mike and I had the time of our lives on this ship. One of the Star Trek doctors hit on me inadvertently in an elevator right in front of both our spouses. I knew the angels had a hand in that flattery. It was a great time. The whole time, my intuition told me that was going to be the last time for a while that all those folks would be on such a great vacation, which lent a touch of nostalgia to the entire event. Like always, it was true.

The day after we got back from the cruise, the whole country shut down, including the ports. I was staying at Mike's house for two nights before returning to my trailer in northern Florida. I had found an inexpensive place to stay long term. It was near my son, whom I visited frequently while I was there. I was kind of expecting Mike and I to reconcile. I still loved him as I always will. We had been very intimate during the cruise and I thought we had grown closer than ever before. Imagine my surprise when the following day he says, "Why don't you stay until Monday so we can go to a notary and have our divorce papers finalized?" I trust the process. I felt this was once again the Universe telling me it was time to go.

On Friday, I had my last appointment with my opiate withdrawal doctor. I had tapered down to the third from the last step in the Zubsolv program. Because of COVID , there was a new protocol where each patient received a pager. I went to wait at the Panera Bread next door. My intuition kept telling me that there would be shortages in medicines. Did I really want to go to a pharmacy to pick up these meds where very likely COVID patients had been? This went on and on for an hour and a half. I finally went back to the doctor's office to see what was going on. I received many apologies. They had forgotten about me. I took that as a sign and said, "There are absolutely no hard feelings. I think I'm going to go. I'm going to quit cold turkey. Thank you, guys, for everything you have done for me. You have many blessings coming your way." And I left.

I believe because I had tapered down so much that my withdrawal symptoms were minor. Three days in a row, I woke up in a panic attack. It was not a pleasant way to wake up. That was it. It was over. It was so surreal not to have to take pills anymore.

Mike and I signed our divorce papers. When I got back to my trailer,

I prayed and said, "God, if you are for real, you will find me a partner." I had been asking my intuition if I had a "one." I was told that in this life-time I am to choose my partner. There are certain souls that are possible ones for me, and out of those I have to choose my one.

Three days later, I met Eric. We bonded because he knew who he was one with, Archangel Michael. I thought he was an empath, as my intuition had not taught me about earth angels yet. This man turned out to be an angel incarnated into mankind. He has no malice in him. He is kind, patient, full of energy, and has the most beautiful blue eyes you have ever seen. We hit it off, spending six, eight hours on the phone. I'm not a phone talker. We decided to meet a few months later in North Carolina, and if that went well, I would move to Pennsylvania, where I currently live. We were instantly comfortable with each other. Every-thing went well.

CHAPTER 23

Pets

A warning for sensitives, pets die in this chapter.

I left this subject for a separate chapter, because so much of my spirituality came through them.

Even my ex-husband, who was a proud atheist, would look at our dog Hinata and say, "I don't believe in God, but when I look at Hinata, I can see the possibility of God being real."

On the day I was born, my parent's cat, a feral calico they couldn't get off their property, gave birth to her litter. My father would tell me the story several times about what a strange coincidence it was. My parents kept the runt of the litter, a small calico cat with markings that most people would consider too ugly to love. Sharing the same birthday was cool. She was never afraid to come up to me, even as a baby. Her name was Mippie. There are pictures of her standing on the tray of my high chair, having beautiful interactions with me. My dad, who was not a cat person, loved her for that.

After moving in together, my parents bought a dog. A Rough Collie identical to Lassie. My father, an American movie buff, was more than happy to name her Lassie. Lassie would lie in front of my crib or playpen and prevent anyone else from getting me out except for my sister, Nicole, or my parents. Any others were greeted with a growl. She was beautiful inside and out. I made more than friends with her. It was like we had a past life connection. My belief is that animals, including dogs, are divine creations and therefore possess an innate spiritual connection, which is why I feel such a powerful attraction towards them. Then one day Lassie got pregnant by a neighbor's German Shepherd who had snuck into our yard. From the litter of six puppies that she had, they decided to keep a female and named her Susie. I was one when Susie was born. Sussie, Lassie, and I were inseparable. I loved them more than any human, including my parents.

When I was four years old, my parents explained that Lassie, our family dog, was sick and needed to go to the veterinarian. One evening, our phone rang and my mom answered. She started crying on the phone. Lassie had passed away. I didn't understand the concept of death yet. It was bewildering to me she would not be back. I started crying hysterically, not because Lassie died, but because I could feel my mother's sorrow. What came next was even worse. My father started crying. I didn't even know grown-ups could cry. I was stunned. Feeling my father's pain was one of the worst experiences of my life. My father, an empath like me, felt deeply, and I was undone by his pain.

To make matters worse, my parents thought it was a good idea to have me watch Lassie movies. They were absolute horror movies to me and it was so bad that I would cry for two or three hours afterwards, until finally one day my mother said, "Ok, that is enough with the Lassie movies."

After Lassie died, Sussie and I became even closer. My parents didn't care what I did as long as I showed up for our two o'clock lunch, which in Spain is the main meal of the day. Sussie and I would get lost on what I called long adventure walks. When I was little, I would spend many hours singing to Sussie because I loved her so much.

When I was eleven, the unthinkable happened. Sussie passed away while my parents were on a visit to the U.S. My sister Karen dropped her off at a vet where she died in a room all alone. When my sister picked me up from school that day, she made me promise to not cry if she told me something. I, of course, a curious child, agreed, and she coldly told me that the love of my life had died. When tears welled up, she threatened me. I was not allowed to cry.

We traveled to the U.S. for our final summer vacation there after Sussie's death, before we relocated permanently. When we got back, something strange happened that would take decades to explain; upon my return, I found Sussie's soul in my cat Mippie.

This might sound odd, but I can sense and identify souls. At that particular moment, I was convinced that I was going insane, but I also knew what I felt. After that, Mippie and I became inseparable, just like me and Sussie were. She was allowed to sleep with me, which Sussie wasn't. Sussie slept in front of my door.

When it came time to move to the U.S., she was on the flight with us in the cargo compartment. I had never experienced flying anxiety before, but this time it was different as I was worried about Mippie. I could feel her anguish and I was not having fun. As soon as I laid my eyes on her sitting in her carrier on the ground of the airport, my heart was filled with joy. We were both over the moon to see each other again. When Nicole arrived to pick us up in our motorhome, the first thing we did was give Mippie a bath. Without any hesitation, Mippie made herself at home by going straight to the couch and falling asleep. I was so relieved.

Appreciated and loved each day of her life, she lived to be seventeen. For approximately six months, I didn't have a pet after she passed. I got really depressed and understood when I found a kitten why. As soon as Pinch arrived, all the gloom and doom were gone. I realized that I would always need a pet in my life.

At one point when I was living in the Scarborough neighborhood, a Chihuahua that was living next door kept coming over every day. We became best friends instantly. "I think she wants to live with you," her owner said. I named her Foxy. She looked so much like a fox that one vet once said she may be part fox. She even had the gangly fox legs and a fox-like tail.

Years earlier when I was working at Aurafin, the jewelry company, a co-worker once said, "You have not been loved until you have been loved by a Chihuahua." She was right. Foxy made me and everyone she met feel like their long-lost dog owner. When she would meet folks, a few would ask, "Are you sure she doesn't want to come live with me? I feel like she is my dog." I would laugh and tell them she did the same thing with everyone. The moment she came into my life, I could hear a voice warning me that she wouldn't live for long and asking if I was sure about taking her in. I once again couldn't help but roll my eyes. I never really believed these things, even though I had no reason not to. What makes telepathy so difficult for me is that when I translate, it comes through as my voice, so often you think you are just being overly worried. Even though I gave my guides the eye roll, I knew in my heart that what I was told was true. I spent every moment I could with Foxy. She even came with me to Las Vegas when I went to deal at the WSOP.

Two years later, Foxy died in my arms of a heart attack. Even though she was an equal opportunity people lover, she was terrified of big dogs. On Easter Sunday, we were adding some pavers to our backyard when she ran out of our backyard. She had an encounter with a Husky that scared her so badly that she had a heart attack and died in my arms. I knew immediately what was going on. I said to Mike, "She is dying."

"Oh, come on, don't exaggerate," was his response. My partner questioning me constantly produced very low self-esteem in me. My biggest obstacle in life is people not believing me. It has led to codependency on drugs because you yourself often feel like you are going crazy. Having a deep spiritual journey is not easy on the psyche.

I stood there for a moment, repeated myself, and took matters into my own hands. We lived across the street from a fire department. I ran to it with Foxy in my arms. The four or five-minute run seemed like hours. I couldn't get there fast enough. I was already inconsolable.

The firefighters hearts were breaking for me. I could feel it. They didn't hesitate and threw her in the back of the ambulance and off we went to the emergency vet. The emergency vet was about fifteen to twenty minutes away. They tried everything they could to revive her. I couldn't stop wailing. Even though I was told she would die young, I was absolutely not prepared for what was happening.

It was as if I had lost my soul mate. I couldn't stop crying. Telepathically, I was told to go online and order a "deer" Chihuahua. What was a deer Chihuahua? Not only did Foxy look distinct from other Chihuahuas, but the ones that resembled her had elongated snouts that were reminiscent of a fawn's, thus the name. The size of deer

Chihuahuas is usually slightly larger than apple head Chihuahuas, which was a plus for me, given that I had small children, and I preferred a Chihuahua that was bigger.

There was one "deer" Chihuahua breeder in Iowa. They were not a recognized AKC breed, so they weren't very popular. But not being AKC also meant a cheaper price tag. Paris Hilton had already made Chihuahuas a thing and AKC Chihuahuas were going between fifteen hundred and three thousand dollars at that time.

There was only one puppy available from that breeder and it was female. My mom always told me to get female dogs because they don't stray. I was over the moon with whom I was going to call Zoe. Zoe was born with an umbilical hernia and had to have surgery, so her arrival was postponed. I paid less than half that of an AKC Chihuahua and waited happily because I was guided to that puppy. She was arriving via cargo airplane. I had to go to the cargo area of Fort Lauderdale airport to pick her up. The cargo area of the Fort Lauderdale Airport was mayhem in 2006. It was like every man for himself. I was just standing there observing and assessing the situation when I saw a dog crate, a nice one, I might add. A little white Chihuahua puppy behind the see-through bars of the door. Folks were just bustling around her. It was a surreal situation. I walked up to the crate and stood there for a few minutes, saying hello. No one bothered me.

Eventually I flagged down someone who looked official, told him I was there to pick up the dog, showed some paperwork and he said "yeah, go ahead, take her." Nothing was entered into any system. Off I went with Zoe. When I got home, I placed the crate in the backyard and opened the door. She came out, tail wagging. I immediately recognized the soul. "What, it can't be. I swear I'm going crazy!" I thought to myself. I was in disbelief. She definitely recognized me! I felt it. What was going on? She walked right up to me and it was like my lifelong dog had just seen me after a long separation. I scooped her up in my arms. As we were walking to my bedroom for a much-needed nap, I asked her out loud, "Are you the reincarnation of Sussie?" and telepathically I heard, "Yes, she is the reincarnation of Sussie, your animal companion for this lifetime and many others."

"Omg, and is this one going to die young also?"

"No, she will be fifteen when she dies." Insert eye roll. I don't know why I always had a hard time believing this stuff. I don't anymore, but it took decades and many miracles to turn this skeptic into a believer. Zoe lived to be fifteen and died on 11/11. For some, that is a very high spiritual day, as 1111 is the ultimate angel number.

Zoe took away any and all pain I had from losing Foxy. Having my childhood dog back was an incredible honor and also left me very perplexed at how it all works. I will tell you this: I have never discounted the fact that all of this could be a Darkside deception. But I cannot discount the fact that these voices have also saved my life numerous times and consoled me when life was breaking my heart.

Zoe exhibited many of the traits Sussie did. Sussie would try to bite any strangers that came onto our property. Zoe did the same. Sussie would thump her tail loudly, so did Zoe. Zoe started experiencing seizures when she was still a pup. My intuition said that it was a side effect of the vaccines she was given and to not take her to the vet for this, that they would take care of it. I was starting to trust this intuition business, so I went with it as an exercise in trust.

We adopted a cat named Jetty shortly afterwards. For years, the kids had been begging for a cat, and it turned out that my mom's good friend's daughter ran a cat rescue in Palm Beach County. Jetty had an overactive thyroid, and I was told the same with her, that they would take care of it. My guides told me to put her on very inexpensive cat food, as that would help her bulk up, so I did. She did grow out of it.

When Zoe was less than a year old, I went to drop off Sabrina at a friend's house for a play date. I was stunned to see a Chihuahua that looked just like Foxy running around unsupervised in the front yard. I said, "Brina, look at that dog, she looks just like Foxy!"

"Oh, that is so and so, my friend's dog," was her response. I started praying the Lord's Prayer and asked if that dog ever had puppies to please make sure I got one.

Years went by. One day Sabrina came home and said, "Do you remember my friend with the Chihuahua? Her dog had puppies. They weren't able to sell one and would like to know if we would like to have her for a hundred dollars rehoming fee?" When Sabrina showed me the picture, I was in shock. I had been looking at her ad on Craigslist several times. No time ever before that had I ever looked at a Chihuahua on Craigslist. I was already being drawn to her. She was a beautiful fawn color, just like Foxy.

This was supposed to be Sabrina's Chihuahua. I made sure not to pet her, feed her, or interact with her. After a few weeks, right before my birthday Sabrina said to me, "It is clear whose dog Hinata really is, so Happy Birthday, mom, she is yours." It was true, despite my best efforts, this dog was in love with me. As soon as we were given the green light, we were hugging and also became inseparable. Zoe and Hinata got along very well, and the three of us were like peas in a pod.

As a child, when I was asked by disembodied voices what my life plans were, the only thing I was sure of was that one day I wanted to have a pack of dogs. It was starting to manifest. Hinata was an amazing dog. She was gaining weight. I was starting a business. I got it in my head to get another dog, a puppy, to play with her. Zoe would play for a few minutes a day, but Hinata wanted to play all day long.

We had already adopted another cat, Boots, whom Noah had domesticated at his grandmother's restaurant one summer. This cat, who was usually timid and afraid of strangers, jumped right up on my lap. I knew she had just adopted me. She was all gray. Boots thought she was a Chihuahua and would even come on our walks with us.

That got me thinking, wouldn't it be cool to have a black Chihuahua? This way we have a white animal, a brown animal, a gray animal, and a black animal in tow. Like the United Nations, all colors coming together. I talked about it with my family and considered getting a puppy from this black Chihuahua litter that was just born. But I kept putting it off. A couple of months later I looked at Craigslist Chihuahuas. There was the most handsome black Chihuahua I had ever seen, a boy. He was mostly black, tri-color to be exact, black, fawn and white. They were looking to rehome him because this couple had just met and one of them had a pit bull. They knew that was not a good mix and also knew that re-homing the Chihuahua was easier, bless their hearts.

When I arrived at our predetermined appointment time, there was no one home and no one answering any texts, phone calls, or emails. Something kept telling me to wait. I never wait. I sat there for over forty-five minutes. Each time I thought about leaving, I would hear "wait," so I waited. I got a panicky phone call from the girl I was meeting saying she was at her girlfriend's and overslept. She would be there within an hour. It was a quarter to one. "Sure," I said, and I sat there playing video games on my phone. Man, was it worth the wait. When that little boy saw me, he ran to me and I to him, like a scene out of a rom-com. He jumped into my arms. When his owner saw this, she cried. I quickly paid her the rehoming fee, and we left, afraid she may change her mind at letting such a wonderful animal go. He slept on my lap the whole way home, like he had known me his whole life. Mr. Spock was just as handsome as in his pictures. He was the best looking Chihuahua I had ever seen. He was about three months old.

After I got him home, I realized that none of the collars that we had fit him. I had such a close connection to him already that I truly felt he didn't need a leash. He came along off leash on our first walk and my intuition was right. He followed all my commands and didn't leave my side.

We had a string of dogs with behavioral issues. I remember clearly looking up at the sky one day and saying, "What have I done to deserve all these difficult dogs? Would it be possible to get a nice one?" That was right before Hinata came to live with us. I couldn't believe my luck. Not only was he handsome, not only did he get along well with my other dogs, but he was obedient as well. The way he looked at me, there was always so much love in his eyes. It was the way Edward looked at Bella in the movie Twilight. Folks would often pick up on this and comment about it.

He was so loving that when he woke up each morning, he would go around and give everyone a good morning kiss. I had never met a soul happier to be alive than Mr. Spock, human or otherwise. He would kiss each of the dogs and whichever humans were around. He was so incredibly happy to be alive that it was contagious. We called him Mr. Happynuts. He was amazing and soon became the love of my life. We were inseparable. He never got very big. He topped out at seven pounds. The first time we spent time apart, on the fourth day, the angels brought his soul to me to show him I was OK. He was so worried about me. What he did is known as astral travel. Our bond was beyond this realm.

I used to ride my bike frequently, covering about five to ten miles, and occasionally up to twenty if I felt like I needed a tougher workout. I got him a harness and he would happily go in there strapped to my chest and off we went on our biking adventures. He absolutely loved it. I even got him a hat because he was a little thin on the top of his head. He was glad to wear it. Once we moved to Pennsylvania, I used the same method to take him hiking with me through the snow.

Mr. Spock kept having near-death or should-have-died experiences. I did begin to wonder if he was being targeted because of me meeting The Creator and all. Things would push him off the top of the stairs and the angels would take over my body or Eric's for perfect midair catches. Hinata was pushed once as well. I was carrying a laundry basket and yet I somehow managed a perfect one-handed catch of an eleven-pound Chihuahua. I used to pray incessantly for his protection.

My intuition suggested that the near-death experiences were attempts to kill him. I kept being told he was holding me back. I kept rolling my eyes. On the morning of February eighth, I woke up not feeling right, like I do so many mornings when something bad was going to happen that day. Though that morning, the sense of dread was particularly fierce. It was early and cold. I let the dogs out. Spock didn't want to go. I forced him. This is so hard to write. After I let him out, I felt death show up and it didn't occur to me to pray to protect him. I have never shared that with anyone. I can't even talk about it. The pain never leaves, you just learn how to live with it.

The love of my life, my beloved Mr. Spock, was run over. He died instantly. When I heard the thump, I knew exactly what it was. As I was walking down the driveway, I heard a voice say, "Catastrophic damage, he died instantly." I heard this two different times. The driver had stopped. I felt so bad for him. Of course, my first concern was his well-being. Then I told him what a difficult path I had already walked and assured him I would overcome this as I was starting to sob uncontrollably. I also asked him that he ask that Spock may reincarnate in peace, which he did. His body was perfectly intact. He had the smallest amount of blood coming out of one nostril. I scooped him up in my arms and brought him into our kitchen. I got on my knees and said, "God, if there is any way that Spock could share Hinata's body and allow both souls to coexist, can you please make it so?" I recited the Lord's Prayer.

I was familiar with human walk-ins. After my awakening, I spent some time helping others with supernatural abilities understand what and who they are. Yahweh would send me a few walk-in cases because I knew what they were and I could help these folks understand themselves better. Walk-ins occur when a soul no longer wants to be here on Earth. No one is kept here, on Earth, against their will. If you really want to die and are sincere, it will be granted. Some souls are offered a deal. If they choose a walk-in instead of suicide, they will incur no karma or sin, if karma or sin are real for them. Knowing this was possible, knowing that God works even closer with animals as they are His creation, I decided to ask to make Spocky a walk-in.

We got confirmation that same night. Mr. Spock had a very peculiar nervous cough. Exactly at midnight, Hinata started coughing that peculiar cough. Her behavior has completely transformed and I have my attentive Mr. Spock back. Which was a good thing because seven months later, I would lose my favorite human of all time, my beloved Skye, as was predicted by me the last time I spoke to her and by my intuition on the playground when I was nine. She did die, three weeks after she turned eighteen.

I absolutely cannot write about that. I am a sensitive after all, and human. Just because I have supernatural abilities, that doesn't mean I'm super human. I am a flawed individual who is just a little different and has different needs.

I have had many adventures since my spiritual awakening. I have experienced even more miracles since then. Alas, I ran out of room to share them in this book, but who knows, maybe someday there will be a sequel.

Afterword

When I finished this book I heard, "That's it, you are done." I invite all of you to see how difficult it was for me to write this book in the afterlife. There were demonic attacks, spirits, and all kinds of things trying to prevent this book from becoming a reality.

Thank you to my brothers and sisters Eric Wickline, Bill Bean, Archbishop Enricht, Jason Mcleod, Anna Estrada, David Litvin, and Kimberly McBride for showing me I am not alone and, of course, for the encouragement.

I don't subscribe to politics or conspiracy theories, but I will leave you with this last message from my intuition: "The Dark Side and the one percent don't want mankind to know folks like these exist."

About the Author

Visit her at Cristina23.com

Cristina Litvin is a spiritual warrior turned writer. Originally from Malaga, Spain, she currently resides in Pennsylvania.

Her work is based on her life experience as she hopes to bring attention to empaths and metaphysics.

When not writing, Cristina enjoys experiencing new places and spending time with her animals.

Milton Keynes UK
Ingram Content Group UK Ltd.
UKHW012313160324
439511UK00013B/411

9 798869 071255